Ivan Pavlov

Exploring the Animal Machine

Owen Gingerich
General Editor

Ivan Pavlov

Exploring the Animal Machine

Daniel Todes

Oxford University Press

For Sarah, with all my love

OXFORD
UNIVERSITY PRESS

Oxford   New York
Athens   Auckland   Bangkok   Bogotá   Buenos Aires   Calcutta
Cape Town   Chennai   Dar es Salaam   Delhi   Florence   Hong Kong   Istanbul
Karachi   Kuala Lumpur   Madrid   Melbourne   Mexico City   Mumbai   Nairobi
Paris   São Paulo   Singapore   Taipei
Tokyo   Toronto   Warsaw
and associated companies in
Berlin   Ibadan

Copyright © 2000 by Daniel Todes
Published by Oxford University Press, Inc.
198 Madison Avenue, New York, New York 10016
www.oup.com

Design: Design Oasis
Layout: Greg Wozney
Picture research: Amla Sanguu

Library of Congress Cataloging-in-Publication Data
Todes, Daniel Philip
Ivan Pavlov: exploring the animal machine / by Daniel Todes.
p. cm. -- (Oxford portraits in science)
Includes bibliographic references and index.
Summary: A biography of the Russian physiologist who won the Nobel Prize for
Medicine in 1904 for research on the digestive system and is perhaps best known
for his research on dogs.
ISBN 0-19-510514-1 (trade: alk. paper)
1. Pavlov, Ivan Petrovich, 1849-1936. 2. Physiologists--Russia (Federation)--
Biography--Juvenile literature. [1. Pavlov, Ivan Petrovich, 1849-1936.
2. Physiologists.] I. Title. II. Series.
QP26.P35 T63 2000
150.19'44'092--dc21
[B]   00-024982

9 8 7 6 5 4 3 2 1

Printed in the United States of America
on acid-free paper

*Frontispiece: Pavlov stands in front of the monument at the Institute of Experimental
Medicine honoring dogs' service to physiology.*
Cover: Pavlov in 1904. Inset: Pavlov with an experimental dog in Sergei Botkin's laboratory.

Contents

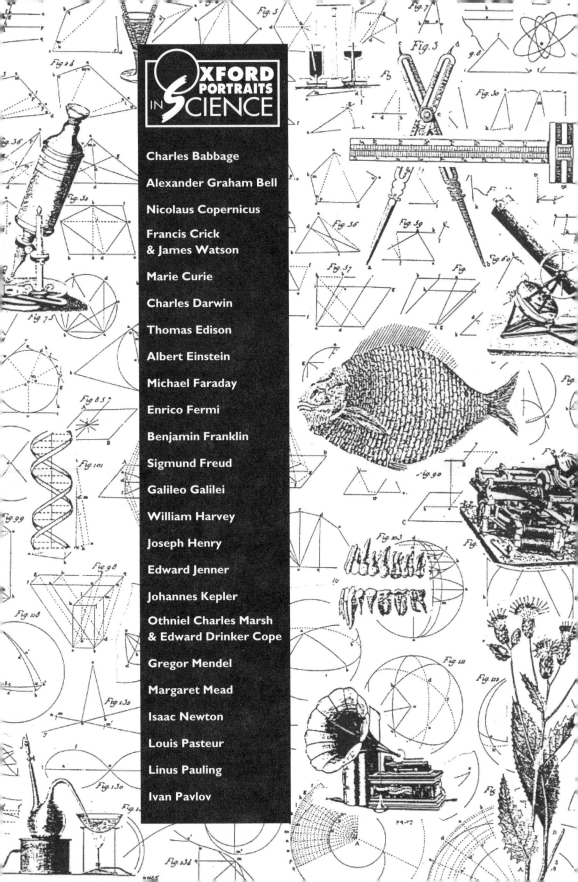

OXFORD PORTRAITS IN SCIENCE

Introduction

When he was 80 years old, Ivan Pavlov plucked an old book off the library shelf, opened it immediately to page 230, and displayed it sentimentally to a friend. The book was George Lewes's *The Physiology of Common Life,* and the page showed a diagram of an animal's internal organs. "When in my very young days I read this book in a Russian translation," Pavlov recalled, "I was greatly intrigued by this picture. I asked myself: How does such a complicated system work?"

"How does such a complicated system work?" That was the question that Ivan Pavlov asked about animals, including humans, throughout his life. How does the heart work, how does the digestive system work, and, finally, how does the brain work? For Pavlov, animals were wonderful and infinitely complex machines that somehow worked precisely as they must in order to survive. The heart surpassed any artificial machine in its ability to pump blood (even regulating its own speed and force) for decades without resting, the stomach adjusted to pour just the right combination of gastric juices on any meal so it could be efficiently digested, and the brain somehow turned the sight of a moving bush into knowledge that an enemy or a potential meal was near.

For Pavlov, these were endlessly fascinating questions—and he loved nothing more than to work on them in his laboratory—but they were also much more than that: the answers would change human history and human nature itself. Knowledge, he believed, was power—and scientific knowledge was the truest and greatest power of all. By fostering an understanding of nature, science would teach

G. H. Lewes's sketch of the internal organs of a mammal, from his The Physiology of Common Life. *Intrigued by this drawing as a teenager in the 1860s, Pavlov still remembered it clearly more than 60 years later.*

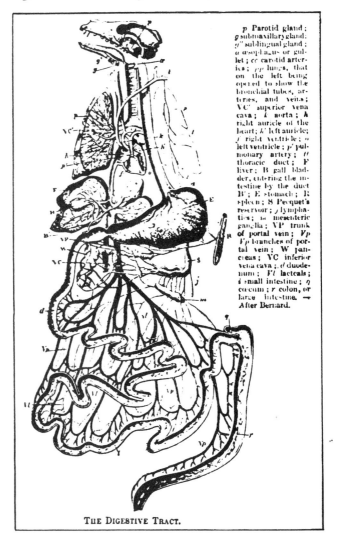

p Parotid gland; g submaxillary gland; g″ sublingual gland; a œsophagus or gullet; cc carotid arteries; pp lungs, that on the left being opened to show the bronchial tubes, arteries, and veins; VC′ superior vena cava; i aorta; h right auricle of the heart; h′ left auricle; j right ventricle; o left ventricle; p′ pulmonary artery; t thoracic duct; F liver; B gall bladder, entering the intestine by the duct B′; E stomach; R spleen; S Pecquet's reservoir; j lymphatics; m mesenteric ganglia; VP trunk of portal vein; Vp V′p branches of portal vein; W pancreas; VC inferior vena cava; d duodenum; F′l lacteals; i small intestine; η cæcum; r colon, or large intestine. — After Bernard.

THE DIGESTIVE TRACT.

humans how to control it; science also would grant humans an unprecedented control over their own lives by giving them a deeper understanding of human nature itself. He put it this way in 1922, after the terrible devastation of World War I: "Only science, exact science about human nature itself, and the most sincere approach to it by the aid of the all-powerful scientific method, will deliver man from his present gloom, and will purge him from his contemporary shame in the sphere of interhuman relations."

Decades after his death, Pavlov remains one of the best-known scientists of the 20th century. For scientists, his pioneering research on digestion, the brain, and behavior still provide important insights and an inspiring example of imaginative experimental techniques. Yet the familiarity of people around the world with Pavlov and his salivating dogs testifies to the broader power of his vision: he has come to symbolize the hope (and for some, the fear) that experimental science might enable us to understand, and perhaps even to control, human nature.

Ivan Pavlov's life, then, is the story of a visionary, a brilliant experimental scientist, and a believer in the power of science to change our world—and ourselves—for the better. It is the story of a long life devoted almost entirely to this single vision. This story begins most improbably: A teenage boy who is studying to be a priest rises early from bed. Glancing about nervously, he walks through the cold dark Russian morning to the new public library. The library is closed, of course—after all, it is five o'clock in the morning—but Ivan has devised a way to sneak in and read some forbidden books.

Pavlov's father, Petr Dmitrievich Pavlov, was a priest and leading member of Ryazan's religious community. He earned extra money by cultivating a family fruit orchard.

The Seminarian Chooses Science

Ivan Petrovich Pavlov would, of course, become a priest. For six generations the Pavlov men had served Russia's Eastern Orthodox Church, slowly making their way up the ladder toward a priesthood. There were few other ways for an ambitious peasant to better his lot. So, in the late 18th century, at the time of Peter the Great, a peasant known only as Pavel became a singer and chanter in a small church in rural Russia. The next three generations of Pavlov men all became priest's assistants. Only in the mid-19th century did the Pavlov family finally break through to the priesthood: Petr Dmitrievich Pavlov and his two brothers—both named Ivan—all graduated from the seminary and received parishes. Petr Dmitrievich (our Ivan's father) was especially fortunate, acquiring the Nikolo-Vysokovskaia Church in Ryazan, a provincial town on the banks of the Oka River in the center of Russia, about 200 miles from Moscow.

Petr Dmitrievich Pavlov was a devout but worldly man, and one of Ryazan's most respected clergymen. Priests in the Eastern Orthodox Church were not paid a salary; instead, they received their rubles and kopeks from parishioners for performing religious services and other priestly

Pavlov's mother, Varvara Ivanovna Pavlova, learned to read despite the opposition of her father, who was an important clergyman in Ryazan.

duties. Petr Dmitrievich supplemented this income with the proceeds of a large fruit and berry garden, and by renting part of his home to students at the local seminary. He was known as a priest who sympathized with the problems of his parishioners, and who would occasionally bend the rules for them. For example, he might grant a couple a church marriage even if they could not provide all of the necessary documents, or if the husband were older or the wife younger than the Church allowed. We know little of his wife, Varvara Ivanovna Pavlova, other than the fact that she was the daughter of a priest, that she bore 10 children, and that Petr considered her a "neurasthenic" (that is, extremely high-strung). As for Varvara's opinion of Petr, we have only the remark of her chief domestic ally, her daughter Lidiia, that Petr ruled the home like a tyrant.

The first of the couple's children was born on September 26, 1849. Ivan Pavlov, recalled one relative, was "a weak and sickly child." Small, frail, and scrawny, he had a phenomenal memory, a passionate nature, and an explosive temper. (Petr blamed this last trait on his wife's hereditary influence.) He did not like to read, and ignored his father's private library—one of the few collections of books available in Ryazan. Ivan preferred to help his father garden and collect berries.

The Pavlovs lived in a comfortable two-story wooden house near the center of Ryazan on Nikolskaia Street. They ate well, but simply. Petr himself prepared meat, flour, vegetables, butter, and sugar for the family table—and a home-brewed beverage that he made from vodka, fruit, and sugar for (moderate) consumption on special occasions.

When Ivan was eight years old, he fell off a high fence onto a stone platform in a neighbor's yard, hurting himself badly. Months passed, but still he did not recover. Finally, his godfather, the Father Superior at a nearby monastery, whisked Ivan away, determined to cure the boy in mind and body. The treatment consisted of discipline, discipline, and more discipline. By day, Ivan worked and played hard— gardening, swimming, skating, or playing *gorodki,* a traditional Russian game that resembles outdoor bowling, but uses a heavy stick instead of a ball. At night, Ivan was locked in an empty room with some books. Out of sheer boredom, the boy began leafing through them, and was soon writing reports for the Father Superior about what he had read. According to family lore, Ivan returned to the Pavlov household a quite different, more studious, and disciplined boy.

RUSSIAN NAMES AND THE PAVLOV FAMILY

There is a little bit of family history in every Russian name. Instead of a middle name, Russians have a "patronymic"—that is, a name based on their father's first name. So, Ivan Petrovich Pavlov was the son of Petr. Ivan's younger brothers, Dmitry Petrovich Pavlov, Petr Petrovich Pavlov, and Sergei Petrovich Pavlov, had the same father as he, and so the same patronymic. The patronymic for a daughter is composed differently. Ivan's sister's name was Lidiia Petrovna Pavlova. The "a" at the end of the patronymic and the family name indicates that Lidiia is female. Likewise, the full names of Ivan's father and mother—Petr Dmitrievich Pavlov and Varvara Ivanovna Pavlova— denote that his two grandfathers were named Dmitry and Ivan. Ivan Pavlov's mother gave birth to 10 children, but only 5 survived beyond childhood. This high infant mortality rate was typical for a Russian family at the time.

Ivan himself would later credit his stay at the monastery for his lifelong appreciation of the importance of a strict schedule that combined hard physical and mental labor.

Aside from his stay at the monastery, two other events from Ivan's childhood had a lasting effect on him: the strange fate of his two uncles, and the Easter holiday.

Petr Dmitrievich's two brothers—Ivan's two Uncle Ivans—had both become priests, but neither was able to keep those positions for very long. One Uncle Ivan became famous for his love of hard drinking and Russian-style brawling—in which the men of an entire street or village fought as a team against those of another. He was soon defrocked for this unpriestly activity and died afterwards from injuries sustained in a fight. The other Uncle Ivan was also a heavy drinker. Soon after he became a priest, life at his church turned very strange. Bodies disappeared from coffins, white-robed figures roamed the graveyard, church bells rang in the middle of the night. One night, the villagers lay in wait to solve the mystery—and nabbed their own priest, Ivan. They beat him severely and left him, drunk and shivering, in the cold. Not surprisingly, he lost his job. The disgraced Uncle Ivan came to live in the Pavlov household and became a favorite companion of the young Ivan. The boy adored his uncle, but he also took the disgrace of his two uncles as a warning—one he would never forget—about the dangers of alcohol and uncontrolled behavior.

Another lasting childhood memory was the Easter holiday. In Ryazan, one day was much like the next—except for Easter and Christmas. The Pavlov family fasted for the 40 days of Lent, living on only toast and *bliny* pancakes. Hungry and weak, they exalted in the holiday days following the great fast. "During the fast," Ivan later recalled, "the weather was gloomy and the church melodies were mournful. Then suddenly there began the bright, joyous Easter with its clear sunny days, with exuberant, cheerful melodies, and with an abundance of tasty treats." In later life—long after he had abandoned his religious faith—Ivan always rejoiced at the Easter holiday and insisted upon celebrating it.

Ivan was tutored at home until he was 11, when he entered the Ryazan Theological School to begin the education that was to prepare him for the priesthood. The curriculum featured rote memorization; the two most important subjects were Latin and Greek, followed by catechism (a formal set of questions and answers about Church doctrine) and biblical history. Within a few years, Ivan became one of the school's best students in all subjects except for singing, in which he performed so poorly that he was excluded from the choir. In 1864, at age 15, he graduated and entered the Ryazan Theological Seminary. Again, he excelled, receiving top grades in a rigorous curriculum that included Church history and dogma, Russian and world history, literature, languages, logic, philosophy, and some courses in the natural sciences. Petr Dmitrievich had every reason to believe that his eldest son would be the first in the seventh generation of Pavlovs to serve the Church.

The times, however, were changing—and Ivan's ideas about how to spend his life were, like those of many other young people, changing with them. To understand what happened next—and why Ivan was sneaking into Ryazan's library in the early morning hours—we need to understand something about Russia during Ivan's teenage years in the 1860s.

At this time, Russia was a huge, desperately poor country with an absolute autocracy and a rigid class structure. The great majority of the population were serfs—peasants, usually very poor, who were legally bound to work on the large estates of the landowners. A serf had no right to move, and indeed very few rights at all. Russia's ruler was the tsar, an absolute monarch whose word was law. From 1825 to 1855, the tsar had been the iron-fisted Nicholas I, whose philosophy was summarized in the slogan: "Autocracy, Orthodoxy, Nationality"—that is, the absolute rule of the tsar, the absolute authority of the Church in spiritual matters, and an unquestioning belief in the national destiny and traditions of the Russian people (as interpreted by the state). Nicholas I tolerated no dissent and tried to keep Western ideas out of Russia. These, he thought, could only cause trouble.

Nicholas I died in 1855 and his successor, Alexander II, had much different ideas. Appalled by Russia's humiliating defeat in the Crimean War (1855–56), Alexander II believed that the country could only become powerful and prosperous if it modernized. The new tsar shook Russian society to its very foundations with his Great Reforms. In 1861, he emancipated the serfs (two years before President Abraham Lincoln's Emancipation Proclamation freed the slaves in the United States). Alexander II reformed Russia's legal and educational systems, relaxed restrictions on travel to the West, and increased people's freedom to form societies and give public lectures. (In each case, however, the government's permission was still needed, even if somebody wanted to form a seemingly nonpolitical society, such as a gymnastics club.) Of course, if these societies and lecturers expressed ideas that the tsar and his officials thought were dangerous, they could still be arrested—but Russians, nevertheless, now had greater freedom than ever before. Alexander II also relaxed censorship restrictions, leading to the publication of many books and the public discussion of many ideas that had earlier been banned.

Russia did not have legal political parties; instead, it had what were called "thick journals." These journals advanced a variety of political views. Radical journals suggested (although subtly, through hints) that Russia should be more like Western countries and should not have a tsar at all. Conservative journals argued that the tsar should be much stricter in crushing dangerous ideas in order to protect Russia's unique traditions and special destiny. These thick journals became the main place where people could read everything from the latest novel (for example, Dostoyevsky's *Crime and Punishment*), to news about the U.S. Civil War, to reports on the latest scientific discoveries. A Russian could tell much about what another Russian thought about the issues of the day by observing the thick journal he preferred. Conservatives read Nikolai Katkov's *The Russian Herald,* while radicals read Nikolay Chernyshevsky's *The Contemporary* and Dmitry Pisarev's *The Russian Word.*

The old Russia, it seemed, was dying; and a new, modern Russia was being born. What would it look like? Discussion circles (called *kruzhki,* the singular is *kruzhok*) sprouted throughout the country, as people read the new literature and gathered to discuss philosophy, politics, literature, and science. "This was a wonderful age," recalled one activist of the time, "an age when every person aspired to think, read, and study. Thought, previously dormant, was awakened and set to work; its impulse was forceful and its tasks titanic. There was no concern for the present; the fate of future generations and the fate of Russia were contemplated."

Such periods of great change affect young people most profoundly. Earlier it had seemed to many youth (at least, to the privileged ones who had a choice) that they would, of course, follow in their parents' footsteps and become, say, landowners, shopkeepers, or priests. But now things were not so clear. What would become of landowners without

The "Tsar-Liberator" Alexander II ruled Russia from 1855 until his assassination in 1881. He freed the serfs, expanded Russia's educational system, and loosened the grip of the state censor.

their serfs? What would happen to the Church? How could one best participate in the building of a new Russia? Many young people rejected family traditions and turned toward a very attractive new alternative: science.

Science became very prestigious in the 1860s for several reasons. The government of Alexander II provided more money for science than ever before, thinking that this would strengthen Russia's economy, technology, military, and medical services. Some of the tsar's ministers also believed that if students were kept busy in scientific laboratories they would have less time and energy for radical political activities. Many intellectuals who opposed the tsarist system also supported science because they considered it the source of new, objective knowledge and a modern belief system—of an alternative to "Autocracy, Orthodoxy, Nationality." Modern science, they thought, offered a materialist worldview. That is, science was explaining everything as a result of the properties of matter and the laws of nature. For these intellectuals, science would free Russians from the superstitious beliefs that bound them to Church and tsar. For example, the scientific explanation of evolution would replace the myth that humans had been created by God, and the scientific study of the human brain would undermine belief in an immaterial and immortal human soul. This was, after all, the age of Charles Darwin's theory of evolution, of developments in chemistry that seemed to eliminate the distinction between life and non life, of the discovery of the law of the conservation of energy, and of almost daily breakthroughs in physiologists' understanding of the human body. The German physiologist Karl Ludwig had even succeeded in keeping a frog's heart beating for many hours outside of its body! And the Russian physiologist Ivan Sechenov had argued, in his controversial book *Reflexes of the Brain* (1863), that all human behavior and thoughts could be explained as the result of machinelike reflex reactions.

Science, then, offered a new, modern faith. "Science,"

one student wrote of the time, "was suddenly elevated to the highest pedestal as if it were a goddess from whom each and everyone had to find a better knowledge to ennoble and improve mankind. Students who were studying to become a high priest of this science had great importance and were viewed as the leadership."

This was the spirit that moved Ivan Pavlov to awake early and hurry to Ryazan's new public library before classes at the seminary began. He and other students had formed a discussion circle to read and discuss the radical thick journals and previously banned books. Seminarians were expressly forbidden to "read books of their own choosing, especially books that include ideas contrary to morality and Church doctrine," so Ivan had to be very careful of the seminary's student inspectors, who roamed the streets of Ryazan looking for misbehaving students. Another problem he faced was that so many people wanted to read Pisarev's essays on science and radicalism in *The Russian Word*, the new Russian translation of Darwin's *Origin of Species,* Sechenov's *Reflexes of the Brain,* and similar works that there was always a long line in front of the library by the time it opened. A member of Pavlov's family later recalled, "When the doors opened, there was a great surge of bodies, and fistfights were a daily event." Many years later, Pavlov confessed that he had finally managed to avoid the mob scene by reaching an agreement with a worker in the library, who left a window open so the determined seminarian could climb in and get his cherished books before the others arrived.

Ivan's passions were now fully engaged. Attending seminary classes by day, he read forbidden literature all night, and, according to one friend, was "the best-read and also the most heated and inexhaustible debater" in his *kruzhok.* He could cite from memory entire pages from Pisarev's articles and from his favorite book—Lewes's *The Physiology of Common Life.* Ivan was especially fond of Pisarev's slogan: "Nature is not a cathedral but a workshop." These words

text continued on page 23

SECHENOV, REFLEXES, AND FREE WILL

van Sechenov was one of Russia's most famous scientists in the 1860s. He was a physiologist who sympathized with the materialist views of the radicals Pisarev and Chernyshevsky. In 1863, he wrote a long article, "Reflexes of the Brain," that used scientific arguments to support radical views. This article was supposed to be published in the radical journal *The Contemporary,* but the government censor would not allow it, so, it was published instead in a medical journal, which the censor thought very few people would read. This medical journal, however, suddenly became very popular, as peo-

Ivan Sechenov, who is known as the "Father of Russian Physiology." He used experiments with frogs to explain human behavior in his controversial tract "Reflexes of the Brain."

ple enthusiastically shared the issue with Sechenov's article. Finally, the censor gave up and allowed Sechenov's article to be published as a book in 1866.

Sechenov argued that even when people believe that they are making decisions—for example, to walk down one road rather than another, to agree with one idea instead of another, to save a drowning person instead of staying safe and dry on the shore—they are actually only doing what reflexes make them do. People, in other words, are not really free. Just as a watch runs in a certain way because of the gears and springs inside it (and a watch can't "decide" to sing a song instead of keep the time), so do people act in a certain way because of reflexes.

For Sechenov, a reflex is a simple process controlled by the nervous system: It consists of a sensory nerve that runs either directly through the spine, or through the brain and the spine, to a motor nerve. The sensory nerve reacts to a stimulus—something in the outside world: for example, a sight, a sound, or a smell. This sends a nervous signal—either directly through the spinal cord or from the brain through the spinal cord—to a motor nerve. The motor nerve moves something—for example, an arm, a leg, or our vocal cords. When a reflex goes from the sensory nerve directly through the spine to a motor nerve, we might make a movement without thinking about it at all. For example, when a doctor strikes your knee with a rubber hammer, you don't think: "I'm going to flex my knee now." You just do it automatically. Sechenov would say: "You do it like a machine."

According to Sechenov, when the reflex from the sensory nerve passes through the brain, you have a thought about what your body is doing. You think that you are doing something on purpose. For example, you recognize a piece of your favorite food (a stimulus has gone from the sensory nerves of your eye to your brain) and you think: "I am going to eat that." Then, you take the food in your hand and put it in your mouth (your brain has sent a signal through the spine to your motor nerves).

Sechenov, though, believed that this thought is itself a reflex—it is an automatic reaction to seeing a food we like. If you see a food you like and do not eat it because it is close to dinnertime and your parents are watching—you are not, according to Sechenov, really making a free decision. Rather, there is a nervous process called inhibition that goes to your brain and says "Don't eat that!" For Sechenov, inhibition is also a reflex. Sechenov thought he had discovered these inhibitory centers in the brain. He argued that our bodies have an enormous number of reflexes and inhibitory mechanisms— and that these together determine everything we do. From the day we are born, all of our experiences—with nature and with our families, teachers, friends, and society—form a network of reflexes and inhibitory responses. Therefore, people who do good things are basically well-built machines; and

text continued on page 22

SECHENOV, REFLEXES, AND FREE WILL

text continued from page 21

people who behave badly are not really to blame—no more than a watch that always runs fast or slow. According to Sechenov, a fair and kind society would train only "good machines"—people who treated one another with respect, who committed no crimes, and always behaved like a real *bogatyr* (the Russian version of a brave and noble knight).

This was a materialist argument based on Sechenov's interpretation of his scientific experiments. For him, the existence of "bad human machines" in Russia was evidence that Russian society needed to be changed. He denied free will and believed that everything that occurs in our minds—all our thoughts and emotions—could be explained by a scientific study of our bodies and environments. Some scientists agreed with Sechenov, and others did not. The Eastern Orthodox Church and supporters of the tsarist system criticized Sechenov's book as bad science with an immoral message. If people had no free will, how could they be held responsible for their actions? Radicals and the young Ivan Pavlov considered it a good scientific argument for building a just society.

When he himself was studying reflexes 60 years later, Pavlov recalled that he had been struck by the "novelty and truthfulness" of Sechenov's "brilliant attempt" to understand thoughts and emotions "in a purely physiological manner."

text continued from page 19

captured the wisdom of the new age: nature should not be worshiped passively as a reflection of God's glory, but rather should be scientifically understood and controlled for the betterment of humankind.

The teachers at the seminary knew, of course, that their students were being influenced by "dangerous ideas." They disagreed, however, about how to deal with this. Some thought the wisest policy was to maintain the traditional curriculum and simply to denounce the spread of materialist and anti-religious ideas. Others believed that seminary classes should study some of the dangerous literature together in order to prepare future priests to combat materialist views. Nikolai Glebov, the priest who taught Ivan's "Logic and Psychology" class, spent much class time refuting "the objections of the materialists against the spirituality of the soul." Another of Pavlov's teachers went even further, and included some books—including Lewes's *The Physiology of Common Life*—that had been criticized by the Church censor. (This teacher, however, was fired.)

Despite his extracurricular studies, Ivan maintained good grades at the seminary (though he was no longer the best in his class) and was careful not to express himself too openly there. The inspector of students would soon attest to Ivan's "good moral temperament," reporting, "I have never noticed in him any ideas contrary to the Christian religion or harmful to the state."

Ivan's thoughts and aspirations, however, had turned decisively elsewhere. In 1869 he told his father that he would not return to the seminary for his final year of study. He was not going to be a priest; rather, he would spend the next year studying for the entrance exams to St. Petersburg University. Petr Dmitrievich was furious, and the breach with his son never really healed. Ivan, however, had made his decision. He would become a priest of the new "goddess"—he was going to become a scientist.

CHAPTER 2

Struggling Scientist in St. Petersburg

The train ride from Ryazan to St. Petersburg took less than a day, but it transported Ivan Pavlov a world away.

Peter the Great, who had founded St. Petersburg at the end of the 17th century, had intended for it to be unlike any other Russian city. In many ways, he had succeeded. This glorious city was home to the tsar, whose Winter Palace stood grandly on the banks of the Neva River. Many canals flowed through the city, and along them stood the great mansions of Russia's nobles. The city was special, not only for its grandeur and beauty, or even because it was the capital of the Russian Empire, but also because it expressed a statement and a hope about Russia's future.

Peter the Great had seen Russia's salvation in the banishing of many old traditions and in making Russia more like the West. This energetic tsar wanted Russia to be a world power, and spent many years in wars with Russia's neighbors. He believed that the tools to modernize Russia were being developed in the West, and, wanting to see these tools for himself, he traveled in disguise throughout the most advanced Western countries. Peter the Great did not want to waste time meeting kings and queens. Instead, he

Tsar Peter the Great's efforts to modernize Russia were felt in every area of life. His reformers are depicted forcing subjects to shorten their beards and coats.

wanted to meet scientists, physicians, and skilled workers who knew how to study nature, heal sickness, build ships, and forge modern weapons. He himself studied carpentry, learned how to pull teeth and perform minor surgery, and looked through one of the first microscopes to see what Antonie van Leeuwenhoek called "little beasties" (microbes). He also brought back with him many Western experts on science and technology, whom he had hired to plant the seeds of their knowledge in Russia.

St. Petersburg was created to be Russia's center for Western ways and scientific knowledge. It was Peter the Great's "window on the West," the new capital of Russia, and the home of his new Academy of Sciences. As a symbol of the direction he wanted to take Russia, he forced Russian nobles to cut off their traditional long beards and to come to his court only when they were clean-shaven in a modern Western fashion.

St. Petersburg, then, had become the acknowledged center of Russian intellectuals, and especially of the country's still small scientific community. The thick journals that took weeks to arrive in Ryazan were written and published here.

Across the Neva River from the tsar's Winter Palace, and next door to the Academy of Sciences, stood Pavlov's destination—St. Petersburg University. The university's science faculty included many of Russia's leading scientists, such as the chemist Dmitry Mendeleyev (creator of the periodic table of the elements we use today), the "Father of Russian Botany," Andrei Beketov, and the controversial physiologist Ivan Sechenov. "The faculty at this time," Pavlov later recalled, "was in a brilliant state. We had a series of professors with enormous scientific authority and with outstanding

Dmitrii Mendeleyev, creator of the periodic table of the elements, was a professor of chemisty at St. Petersburg University during the time that Pavlov was a student there.

talent as lecturers." With Lewes and Sechenov no doubt much on his mind, Pavlov chose as his specialty the physiology of animals and, typically, threw himself passionately into his studies.

Life in the big city was very hard, however, on both Pavlov and Nikolai Bystrov, his good friend from the seminary who had also entered the university. They were living on a small student stipend and trying to cope with a very different environment and rigorous university studies. Bystrov suffered a nervous breakdown and soon returned to Ryazan. In April 1871, toward the end of his first year at the university, Ivan also developed problems. He was diagnosed with a "disturbance of the nerves" and returned to Ryazan in mid-May, without taking the exams for promotion to the second year.

He recuperated over the summer and returned to St. Petersburg in mid-August, accompanied by his younger brother Dmitry. Dmitry had always looked after Ivan in Ryazan, and he now did the same in St. Petersburg, sewing torn buttons back onto his coat, finding a decent apartment,

The "Bronze Horseman" statue of Peter the Great stands in front of the Senate building in St. Petersburg. The tsar moved Russia's capital from Moscow to his new "window on the West," which he named after the Christian apostle St. Peter.

As a student at St. Petersburg University, Pavlov adopted physiology as his specialty. He needed an extra year to complete college, due to his "nervous exhaustion" one year and the extra time he devoted to his scientific research in others.

locating a cafeteria with edible food that was affordable on a student stipend, and so forth. Dmitry also entered St. Petersburg University, where he studied chemistry with the famous Mendeleyev. A charming and gregarious fellow, he soon made the Pavlov apartment a comfortable social center for Ivan and his friends. For the rest of his life, Ivan would always have somebody to look after him in this way, which he apparently needed to live and work productively.

Ivan now easily passed his first-year exams and devoted his time solely to his new *kruzhok* (his informal discussion circle) and to university studies. If he had hoped to study with Sechenov, though, he was disappointed. The famous physiologist had resigned after quarreling with university authorities.

The new professor of physiology was a brilliant, strange, and ill-fated physiologist only six years older than Pavlov himself: Ilya Fadeevich Tsion. Tsion mentored Pavlov for only two years, but, as Pavlov put it many years later, "Such a teacher is not forgotten throughout one's entire life." Pavlov recalled that he and the other aspiring young physiologists "were simply astounded by Tsion's masterful, simple presentation of the most complex physiological questions and his truly artistic ability to perform experiments."

There are many different ways for a scientist to study an animal, and physiologists at this time took a number of approaches. Some physiologists held a "reductionist" view, believing that the best way to study an animal was by reducing it to its simplest, most basic part, which they thought at this time was the cell. Since animals are just groups of cells, they reasoned, once scientists understood how the cell worked, they could easily understand the entire animal as well. Other physiologists went even further. For them, cells were nothing more than atoms and chemicals, so the physiologist should really be a combination of a physicist and a chemist.

Tsion disagreed with this reductionist approach. Like his own teacher, the great French physiologist Claude Bernard, he thought the physiologist should concentrate on a "higher" level and should study animal organs (for example, the heart, the digestive system, and the brain). These organs, after all, performed the basic functions in the animal body—circulating the blood, digesting food, generating thoughts and emotions, and so on. So, to understand these processes, the physiologist should begin with these organs. Chemistry and physics could certainly help the physiologist do this, but they could not (at least in the forseeable future) answer the basic questions about what made an animal tick: that is, about how it kept the blood flowing throughout its body, how it turned food into energy, and how it learned about and responded to its environment.

But how could the physiologist study animal organs? Tsion's answer, like Bernard's, was: through vivisection (the dissection of living organisms) and experimentation. If the physiologist wanted to know, for example, what nerve controlled the heartbeat, the way to do it was to operate on an animal, cut the nerves that might control the heartbeat, and observe the results. Sechenov had not been able to bear the sight of blood and had only very reluctantly performed vivisection on live animals—limiting himself to the relatively lowly frog. Tsion, however, showed his students how to perform vivisection experiments on larger mammals that more closely resembled humans—namely, rabbits, cats, and dogs. This required not only steely nerves, but also good surgical technique.

Pavlov later recounted one anecdote about his mentor that had especially impressed him. Tsion loved high society and formal occasions. One day, he discovered that he had mistakenly scheduled an important vivisection for an evening in which he had been invited to a fancy-dress ball. Unwilling either to skip the ball or postpone the dissection, he arrived in the laboratory dressed in a coat, top hat, and white gloves. Without even removing his gloves, he hurriedly performed a complex operation on the stomach of the experimental animal. When he had completed the operation and rushed out the door to his party, both the gloves and his shirtfront were spotless—dramatic testimony to his surgical virtuosity. Under Tsion's instruction, Pavlov too became an expert surgeon. It helped that the young student was ambidextrous—that is, he was equally adept with both hands, and could cut as easily with either during operations.

As a college student, then, Pavlov worked closely with

Students in the dining room at St. Petersburg University in 1910.

Tsion, attending his lectures on physiology and spending most evenings in Tsion's small physiology laboratory. Like his teacher, Pavlov studied the digestive organs and the heart. Even before graduating from college, he presented the results of his experiments to St. Petersburg's scientific community. For one of these reports, Pavlov was awarded a gold medal in a university competition. He spent so much time on his scientific experiments, however, that he needed an extra year to finish his required courses and graduate from college.

Pavlov now knew for certain that he wanted to be a physiologist. He also knew that he would have a much better chance to get one of the rare jobs as a professor of physiology if he first graduated from medical school. So, he decided that after college he would go to Russia's best medical school, St. Petersburg's Military-Medical Academy. Tsion was now a professor there as well, and he invited his prize student to serve as his laboratory assistant there. Everything, it seemed, was going very well.

A disaster, however, soon intervened. As Pavlov recalled bitterly many years later: "There occurred a wild episode and this most talented physiologist, Tsion, was chased out of the Academy." Tsion's career was destroyed and Pavlov was deprived of his beloved teacher. How could a professor be "chased out" of his job? The answer reminds us that science and teaching are done by real people and can cause great controversy and strong emotions.

Many people disliked Tsion, and they had many different reasons for doing so. For one thing, he had an abrasive personality and struck many people as arrogant and cold. Radicals and liberals did not like him because he disagreed with them about the need to change Russia's existing social and economic order, and because he rejected Sechenov's ideas about materialism. Tsion believed that physiologists could never discover how thoughts and emotions were connected to the purely physical processes in our bodies—let alone whether or not there existed a soul or free will. Thoughts and emotions, after all, were not something physical—not something one could see or touch. How could they possibly be studied in a truly scientific way? In his lectures and articles, Tsion criticized Sechenov and everybody else who considered physiology a "materialist, radical science." (Tsion also convinced the young Ivan Pavlov to abandon, at least for a while, his interest in these subjects and to concentrate instead on studies of the heart and digestive system.) Radical and liberal journals published articles accusing Tsion of being a bad scientist and a dishonest man.

Many conservatives, who liked Tsion's political views, did not support him because he was Jewish. Anti-Semitism was a powerful force in Russia, and Tsion was one of the first two Jewish professors in Russian universities. Finally, many students in his medical school class resented Tsion because he was a hard grader. Most professors at the Military-Medical Academy guaranteed all their students a C-grade, regardless of their performance on tests. Tsion, however, refused to do so, and he failed more than 100 students in his course on physiology.

For all these reasons, students organized demonstrations against Tsion and many people supported their demand that he be fired. When he attempted to deliver a lecture, angry students pelted him with eggs and cucumbers. At first, the government supported the embattled professor, arresting student demonstrators and even stationing armed guards in his lecture hall to preserve order. In the fall of 1874, however, the demonstrations spread, closing down St. Petersburg University, the Military-Medical Academy, and the city's other institutions of higher education. Tsion's support evaporated. Government officials asked him to take a "vacation"—and never invited him back.

For Pavlov, of course, this was a catastrophe. His beloved teacher had been humiliated and destroyed, and his own plans shattered. Even 50 years later he recalled that, as one of

Tsion's few defenders, he had been treated by other students as "almost a spy." Fiercely loyal, he refused to work with the new professor of physiology who replaced Tsion. He even boycotted the university ceremony during which he was to receive the gold medal he had won for his scientific work in Tsion's laboratory.

The next 15 years were very difficult. Pavlov completed medical school (1880) and then advanced studies in medicine (1883) without a mentor to guide him. Although he published many articles about the heart and digestive system, the few vacancies for a professor in physiology went to other candidates who had the support of powerful professors. At one point, he became so depressed that he thought he was dying. Three very important positive things occurred in his life during these years, however, and sustained him for better times.

The first was meeting Serafima Vasil'evna Karchevskaia, a young woman who, like Ivan, had followed the currents of the time from a provincial city to the great capital of St. Petersburg. Serafima's father had died when she was 10, and she and her four siblings were raised by her mother, the principal of a small school. Serafima had begun earning money as a tutor when she was 10, which did not prevent her from also being an excellent student. Unlike Ivan, Serafima was unimpressed by Pisarev and materialism—she remained a religious young woman. Yet she, too, was influenced by the radical ideas of the day—especially by the demand for women's equality, which encouraged her to defy social conventions and pursue a career.

In the 1870s, there was another widespread social movement in Russia: the movement to "go to the people." Many educated young people became convinced that it was selfish to think only of their own careers when so many people in Russia were poor, hungry, and illiterate. They decided, instead, to use their skills to help the overwhelming majority of the population—the poor peasants. Many young physicians left for the countryside to practice medicine in peasant villages, and many young teachers decided to spend their lives teaching peasants how to read. (The great Russian writer Anton Chekhov joined this movement, and many of his stories are about physicians like himself who practiced medicine in the impoverished countryside.) Like Ivan's father, Serafima's mother did not want her to leave home, but the independent young woman left for St. Petersburg in 1878 to enroll in the Teaching Courses for Women and, afterwards, to "go to the people." While in St. Petersburg, Serafima organized many events to raise money for poor students, including a public reading by the great novelists Fyodor Dostoyevsky and Ivan Turgenev.

In 1879, Serafima and Ivan were introduced by a mutual friend. They liked each other almost immediately, but Ivan was too shy to ask her for a date. (He was also under the

Serafima and Ivan shortly after their marriage. Ivan's brother Dmitry worried that the marriage might not last, since each, he thought, was accustomed to being pampered.

mistaken impression that Serafima was from a rich family, and so feared she would look down on him.) So, he waited until she was about to go home for the summer, and asked permission to write her letters. She agreed, and he soon began sending her a journal that he wrote and entitled *Trapped*. Here the shy young man poured out all his thoughts and feelings about life, literature, science, and current events. She responded with letter after letter. When she returned to St. Petersburg in the fall, the pair became inseparable. They soon decided to marry, but postponed the wedding until 1881. Serafima first spent a year in the countryside fulfilling her mission to "go to the people." Ivan was supposed to finish his doctoral dissertation, but (as often happens with big projects) this took much longer than he expected. He completed it two years after he married, in 1883.

The young, idealistic couple discussed everything on their minds: the nature of true love, Dostoyevsky's latest novel, scientific discoveries, and the events of the day. Both were horrified when, in 1881, Alexander II—who had done so much to change Russia—was assassinated by a terrorist bomb as he rode in his carriage through St. Petersburg.

When they were apart during the years before their marriage, they corresponded almost every day. Ivan's letters to Serafima tell us much about his personality and aspirations. He confessed that he was overly sensitive to insults (real and imagined), that he had "attacks of nastiness," and at times felt somehow separated from other people. He described his great strength as a commitment to honesty and truth, which were "for me a kind of God." He also wrote, "However things might change, what is important to me is my own consciousness of the rightness of my behavior."

Becoming a scientist, he explained to Serafima, was for him not only a way of searching for truth, but also of learning how to think properly. When he was younger, he recalled, he would argue passionately for hours about subjects about which he really knew very little. Now he was trying to develop a "mature mind." Real truths were difficult to obtain. One could find them only by becoming an expert in a specialized, even narrow field, by being passionately interested in that field, and by the scientific process of experiment, checking, and rechecking. As he described it, "To think is to persistently investigate a subject, to have it always on one's mind, to write, to speak, to argue about it, to approach it from one and the other angle, to gather all the reasons for one or another opinion about it, to eliminate all objections, to recognize gaps where they exist." In short, one must "experience the joy and grief of serious intellectual effort." The best place to learn how to think was a scientific laboratory, which Pavlov called "a school for brains."

Pavlov had not surrendered Sechenov's old dream of understanding how the brain formed thoughts and emotions, but he doubted that real experimental science was ready to tackle such a complicated subject. "Where is the science of human life?" he wrote to Serafima. "Not even a trace of it exists. It will exist, of course, but not soon, not soon."

During the first 10 years of their marriage, the devoted couple encountered many difficulties and one great tragedy. They had very little money. Sometimes they lived with Ivan's brother Dmitry, and sometimes they rented an apartment in the poorest section of the city. Serafima once awoke to find their newborn son, Vladimir, covered in lice. Shortly thereafter, the couple decided that it would be both healthier and less expensive for Serafima and Vladimir to live in the countryside with Serafima's sister. There young Vladimir suddenly took ill and died. Both parents, of course, were grief-stricken. Ivan lost himself in his work. Serafima turned fervently to the Eastern Orthodox Church, spending day after day in constant prayer. A second son—whom they also named Vladimir—was born two years later.

Ivan earned what money he could by giving lectures

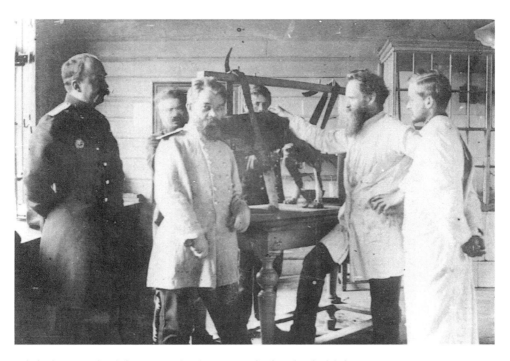

while he searched for a good job. One job that he held from 1878 to 1890 paid very little money, but turned out eventually to be a stroke of good fortune. Sergei Botkin, the professor of medicine at the Military-Medical Academy and personal physician to the tsar's wife, decided to create a small laboratory to test how various medicines affected animals. Botkin himself was too busy to run the laboratory and asked a young physician for advice about whom to hire. The physician recommended his good friend Ivan Pavlov. So, Pavlov supervised research in Botkin's laboratory and also used the facilities for his own research. One advantage of this job was that, when Serafima became ill, she enjoyed the medical services of the physician to the tsarist family. Another was that Pavlov gained important experience in running a laboratory. Finally, Botkin introduced Pavlov to a number of very influential people.

Another positive event of these troubled years was Ivan's and Serafima's two-year trip to western Europe. In 1884, Ivan was one of three students who won a competition for a

Pavlov (second from the right) in Botkin's laboratory at the Military-Medical Academy. Supervising Botkin's experiments gave Pavlov access to facilities for his own research.

scholarship to continue their scientific studies in the West. Ivan used the money to travel to Germany and study with two of the leading physiologists of the time, Rudolf Heidenhain and Karl Ludwig. He was able to exchange ideas with both about their common interest in the heart and digestive system. Even more important, Ivan learned how two of Europe's best laboratories were organized. Heidenhain and, especially, Ludwig did not work alone in a small room or two. Rather, they had many assistants and all sorts of modern equipment. This allowed them to work much more efficiently than did the scientists in the poorer Russian laboratories that Pavlov had known.

Any work is difficult to do well if one does not have the proper tools, and science is no exception. Toward the end of the 1880s, Pavlov become increasingly frustrated with one particular problem with the tools in Botkin's laboratory: it was difficult or impossible there to experiment on "normal" animals. Pavlov's frustration was based on his own idea about how physiologists could best discover how animal machines worked.

For Pavlov, physiologists could conduct either "acute" or "chronic" experiments. Each type of experiment produced a different kind of knowledge. In an acute experiment, the physiologist operated on an animal in some way and immediately observed the results. For example, a physiologist who wanted to know what happened to food in an animal's stomach would feed an animal, wait a certain amount of time, and then cut the animal open and observe its stomach contents. During such acute experiments, of course, the animal was often bleeding and writhing in pain—or it was given a drug to keep it quiet. In either case, Pavlov thought, much of what the physiologist saw during the experiment was the result of the operation itself. Animals were very complex machines, and so the pain and trauma of an operation no doubt affected all its life processes. An acute experiment, then, was like smashing a watch with a hammer in order to see how its gears and springs worked. The scientist could find out something about the individual parts of an animal this way—about the shape of its "gears and springs"—but could not see how these parts worked together when a normal, functioning animal actually breathed or digested food.

But how could a physiologist experiment on a normal, functioning animal in order to discover how it really worked? For Pavlov, the answer was the "chronic experiment." The main idea in a "chronic experiment" was to use surgical means to change the animal into a sort of living experimental tool. The physiologist did this by first performing an operation to either implant or change something in the animal. The animal then was allowed to recover from the operation, just like any human patient who had undergone surgery. Only after the animal had recovered, did the physiologist begin the experiment.

For example, in 1889 Pavlov and his collaborator, Ekaterina Shumova-Simonovskaia, wanted to know what caused the gastric glands in the stomach to secrete gastric juice (gastric juice is the liquid that digests food in the stomach) when the animal eats. Other scientists had studied this question and concluded that the physical pressure of food in the stomach caused the glands to produce gastric juice. Pavlov disagreed. He thought that appetite—the animal's desire for food and the pleasure it received from eating—made the gastric juices flow even before food actually reached the stomach. But how could he test this?

Pavlov's solution was to operate on a dog to implant a gastric fistula and to perform an esophagotomy. The gastric fistula is a thin tube that runs from the inside of the stomach to the outside of the body. Any gastric juice that the stomach produces runs out through the tube, and the experimenter can then collect the juice in a bottle and analyze it. An esophagotomy, a more complicated (and, you might think, diabolical) operation, separates the animal's mouth

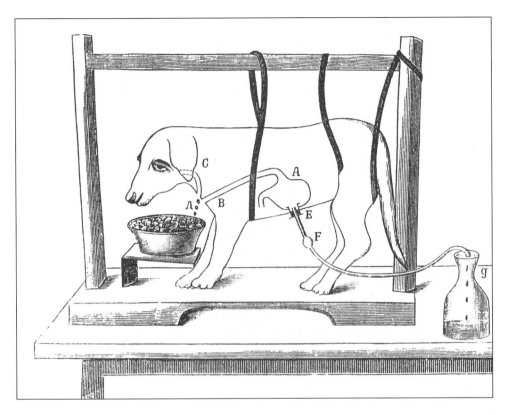

Pavlov demonstrated the role of appetite in digestion by using a dog with a gastric fistula and esophagotomy. In this diagram from a 1907 Russian medical journal, the dog eats the food, which falls out of an aperture (C) in the neck—and so never reaches the stomach. Yet "appetite juice" flows out of the gastric fistula (E).

cavity from its digestive tract. When the animal eats a piece of food, the food falls out through a hole instead of reaching its stomach. As a result, the animal enjoys eating the food, but the food never reaches its stomach.

Pavlov performed these operations on dogs, waited for them to recover from the operations, and only then began his experiments. He discovered that even though the food these dogs ate never reached the stomach, the gastric glands produced a great mass of "appetite juice"—that is, gastric juice produced by the influence of appetite.

By using a chronic experiment, Pavlov had proven his point. He criticized scientists who had used acute experiments to deny that appetite caused the production of gastric juice. According to Pavlov, these scientists had been fooled by the problems in an acute experiment. He wrote that a dog that is bleeding, in pain, or drugged is not going to experience pleasure while it eats, so, of course, it does not produce any "appetite juice." But this did not really tell physiologists what happened when a normal dog ate—it only meant that the physiologist's acute experiment had smashed some of the "gears and springs" in the animal machine.

The problem for Pavlov was that these operations and other, even more complicated ones, could only be successful if a laboratory had the necessary equipment and was clean enough for the dog to recover from surgery. The Botkin laboratory was small and poorly equipped—if Pavlov needed any special tools, he had to make them himself. More important, the hygienic conditions were "nasty," according to Pavlov, and so most of the dogs and rabbits died from infections after any complex operation. "So, it's not my fault," he wrote to Serafima in 1882 about the slow progress on his dissertation. "I'll take up other experiments that do not require the animals upon which I operate to remain alive."

We must remember that, at this time, scientists were just beginning to accept what seemed to be an unlikely idea: that tiny, even invisible germs could kill large animals. Even people who operated on humans were still debating how clean they needed to keep an operating room and how to do this. It was not unusual for a surgeon to stick an unwashed finger into a patient's wound to see how it was healing. So, not a single physiology laboratory in the world took the extensive measures that Pavlov thought were necessary for an experimental animal to regularly survive a complex operation. These measures were necessary for Pavlov's favorite style of physiology—for chronic experiments—but he simply did not have the resources or facilities to study physiology in the way that he wanted.

By the time he was 40 years old, then, Pavlov had many good ideas but was also very frustrated. He had very little money and had twice been turned down by Russian universities when he applied for a job as professor. Many of the physiology experiments he wanted to perform were simply impossible in Botkin's laboratory, and precious time was slipping away. As he wrote at the time: "My time and strength are not spent as productively as they should, because it is not at all the same to work alone in somebody else's laboratory as to work with students in one's own laboratory."

At the time he wrote these words, he could not have known that an unlikely series of events was about to utterly change his professional life. This process began in 1885 when a rabid dog named Pluto bit a military officer in St. Petersburg. Rabies is a terrible disease, and, until that year, it had always been fatal. In 1885, however, the bacteriologist Louis Pasteur, who lived and worked in Paris, announced that he had developed a rabies vaccine. Fortunately for Pluto's victim, his commanding officer was Prince Aleksandr Petrovich Oldenburgskii. The prince was a wealthy man, a cousin of Alexander III, and very interested in science and medicine. He not only sent his officer to Paris for treatment, but decided to create a facility in which Russia could produce its own vaccine. A few years later, the Pasteur Institute—a modern scientific center where Louis Pasteur could continue his bacteriological studies—was founded. Inspired by that example, Prince Oldenburgskii decided to use his own money to establish Russia's first institution devoted to medical research.

The prince appointed some of Russia's leading medical scientists and physicians to a committee that would help plan his Institute of Experimental Medicine. He also included Ivan Pavlov, probably because of Pavlov's close relationship to the tsar's wife's physician, the very influential Professor Sergei Botkin. The prince originally had intended to appoint another Russian physiologist—who was more famous and respected than Pavlov—as the head of the institute's physiology division. Many people concluded, however, that the prince knew too little about medical science and that any institute he controlled would, therefore, fail. His leading advisors resigned, and many scientists refused his offer of a job. Finally, in part because of Pavlov's help on the organizing committee, Prince Oldenburgskii made him chief of the institute's physiology division.

Just two years earlier, Pavlov had been rejected for two jobs as a professor. Now, in 1891, he had unexpectedly become chief of Russia's largest and most modern physiology laboratory. The 1880s had been a very difficult decade; the 1890s would prove to be a triumphant one.

Pavlov lecturing to medical students at the Military-Medical Academy. His lectures featured experimental demon-strations, using special dogs accustomed to the large audience.

Pavlov's Physiology Factory

For the first time in his life, Pavlov now had the resources he needed to support his family and pursue his scientific interests as he saw fit.

Aside from receiving a very good salary from Prince Oldenburgskii's Institute of Experimental Medicine, he was also appointed to a professorship at the Military-Medical Academy. The Pavlov family was able to pay off its debts and move to a spacious apartment just around the corner from the Academy of Sciences. Serafima abandoned her career as a teacher and settled into the traditional life of the wife of a successful professor. As Ivan's career blossomed, Serafima gave birth to three more children (Vera in 1890, Viktor in 1892, and Vsevolod in 1893). She also did for Ivan what his brother Dmitry had done years before: she handled all the business of life so he could concentrate on his science. Her household jobs included managing their financial affairs, as Ivan proved to be totally incompetent (or just totally uninterested) in handling them.

In these years, Serafima spent an increasing amount of time in church. Only her renewed religious faith, she confided in a letter to a friend, had "saved me from going out of my mind" after the death of her first son. She now tried to convince Ivan to accompany her to church services, but without success. He remained true to Pisarev and 1860s materialism. Ivan respected the cultural role of religion (and he defended freedom of religion when it came under attack in later years), but he did not believe in God or in any religious doctrines. He considered those who did to be "weak types" incapable of facing life without superstition. Despite this difference in their outlook, Ivan and Serafima enjoyed the first fruits of success after the very difficult 1880s. Serafima later remembered the 1890s as "the happiest years ever."

Pavlov now adopted a regular, work-centered routine: He awoke at about seven-thirty in the morning, ate a light breakfast, and dashed off to his laboratory at the institute or to the Military-Medical Academy, on days that he lectured to medical students there. He worked in his laboratory until about six o'clock, when he went home for dinner. After dinner, he took a nap. Waking at about eight-thirty, he relaxed in the dining room, where he drank tea and listened to music. Later in the evening, when his family retired to bed, he went to his study to write. He liked to go to sleep late, at about one o'clock in the morning. In later years, when he supervised research in three different laboratories, he changed this routine a bit. He would return home for lunch on particular days and spend some time either listening to music or admiring his art collection before returning to work. Pavlov also made time for regular physical exercise. He founded a gymnastics club, rode a bicycle, and enjoyed cross-country skiing. He always walked very briskly through St. Petersburg on his path between his three laboratories and home. His routine was so strict that when somebody wanted an unscheduled talk with him, he would often tell them that he had time only during these walks. Many people found it very difficult to keep up with his fast pace (perhaps Pavlov used this to discourage people from wasting his time, which he considered very precious).

Two unexpected strokes of good fortune made Pavlov's laboratory at the institute an especially good place to do his research. First, many people came there in order to work with him. They came, not because Pavlov was famous (he was not), but rather because of a specific government policy. The great majority of Russian physicians worked for the government—and most of these worked for the military. Keeping soldiers healthy and healing their wounds was an important priority for any army. Most physicians at this time had very little scientific training, and the government thought that doctors could do their job better if they learned to "think scientifically."

Therefore, the government decided that it would pay for any doctor to spend two years taking science courses and working in a laboratory. If the physician then completed a research project and wrote a doctoral dissertation he would get a much higher salary, a better job, and other privileges. (There were very few women physicians in Russia at the time.) So, the people who came to Pavlov's laboratory knew very little about physiology. More than anything, they usually wanted Pavlov to help them identify and finish a research project in a very short time. In the years 1891 to 1904, about 100 of these coworkers passed through Pavlov's laboratory. With Pavlov's help, most of them were able to finish their dissertations and build very successful medical careers.

This arrangement also worked very well for Pavlov. He had many ideas for research projects, but only two hands, so he was happy to have so many people to help with his research. Pavlov called these coworkers his "skilled hands." He himself usually provided the "head." Pavlov and a few experienced assistants would operate on a dog, tell the coworkers what to do with it afterwards, supervise their experiments, and interpret the results. Pavlov's "skilled hands" performed thousands of experiments on hundreds of dogs—giving Pavlov's creative "head" much more information to work with than if he had been working alone.

This way of organizing laboratory work very much resembled the production process in factories during this period. Pavlov was a very strict manager. If his "skilled hands" did not do their work precisely the way the chief wanted, the experiments they performed would be of no value. Therefore, he tested the new workers for a month or two before he assigned them a research topic (and he gave the most important topics to the workers he thought were best). He demanded punctuality and precision. As one coworker put it, "the laboratory worked like the mechanism of a watch."

Every morning when Pavlov arrived at the laboratory, he checked the coat-rack. If any coworker was late (as evidenced by the absence of his coat), he faced Pavlov's explo-

Pavlov (center) and his coworkers operate on a dog in the surgical complex on the second floor of his laboratory at the Imperial Institute of Experimental Medicine.

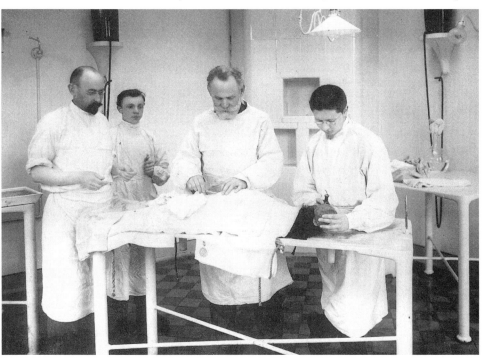

sive temper. One coworker left this description of Pavlov's dramatic entrance in the morning: "When he entered, or, more correctly, ran into the laboratory, there streamed in with him force and energy. The laboratory literally enlivened, and this heightened tone and work tempo was maintained until his departure. He brought to the laboratory his entire personality, both his ideas and his moods. He discussed with all his coworkers everything that came into his mind. He loved arguments and arguers, and would egg them on."

Pavlov would wander through the laboratory, supervising the experiments of his coworkers. Sometimes he would pick up the notebook in which a coworker kept the protocols (the results of experiments) and test the coworker to see if he knew exactly what the results had been. If he did not, or if he had conducted experiments carelessly, Pavlov "would hurl himself upon the guilty party and criticize him sharply." Pavlov organized discussions in the laboratory, during which all the coworkers would share their results and ideas. Anybody could disagree with Pavlov's ideas. No secrets were permitted. Finally, when the coworker had completed his experiments and written his thesis, he would read it aloud to Pavlov. The chief would analyze every result and idea—and if there was some problem, he demanded that new experiments be conducted. In these ways, the laboratory's "head" constantly guided the activity of his "skilled hands."

With all these new coworkers, Pavlov's laboratory quickly became very crowded—until the second stroke of luck occurred. In 1893, the philanthropist Alfred Nobel (who had made a fortune through his discovery of dynamite) donated enough money for Pavlov to double the size of his laboratory. Again, Pavlov proved to be the right person in the right place at the right time. Nobel was getting old and sick, and he hoped that physiologists would study his particular health problems, which included digestive

The two-story stone laboratory building financed by Alfred Nobel's gift. On the far right is Pavlov's wing of the building, in which all scientific divisions were originally housed.

problems and a general decline in vitality. Perhaps, he wrote in the letter that accompanied his donation, the institute would perform experiments to see if the digestive system from a healthy animal could be transplanted into the body of a sick one, or if transfusing the blood from a healthy animal (Nobel suggested a giraffe) would cure a sick one. Pavlov attempted to implement Nobel's second idea by sewing together the circulatory systems of two dogs. This repeatedly failed, however, and he abandoned the project.

Pavlov used Nobel's money to build precisely the kind of laboratory he wanted. This two-story stone building had a kennel in the basement, three rooms for experiments on the first floor, and a surgical and recovery complex for experimental animals on the second floor. Pavlov was especially proud of the second floor, which he called the world's first "special operative division in a physiological laboratory." This surgical complex was carefully designed so that dogs could be operated upon and recover for chronic experiments. Dogs were washed and dried in one room, prepared for surgery in a second, and operated upon in a third. A separate room was devoted to the sterilization of instruments, the washing of the operator's hands, and the donning of clean clothes. Next to the surgery room were individual recovery rooms for dogs. In other words, Pavlov's dogs were operated upon and cared for almost as if they were human patients in a good hospital.

Why did Pavlov experiment upon dogs, rather than upon some other animal? For one thing, he wanted to use a mammal that had a digestive system resembling that of humans, and one that could be acquired relatively easily and at low cost. Pavlov found that rabbits often died after surgical operations and that pigs were too "nervous and sensitive" for "physiological experiments requiring calm." He thoroughly disliked cats, which he once termed "loud and malicious animals." He spoke of the dog, on the other hand,

A laboratory room at the entrance to the surgical and recovery complex, which Pavlov called the world's first "special operative division in a physiological laboratory."

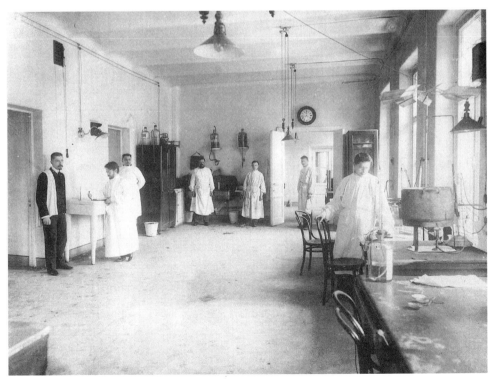

as the experimenter's ideal partner: "We must painfully acknowledge that, precisely because of its great intellectual development, the best of man's domesticated animals—the dog—most often becomes the victim of physiological experiments. During chronic experiments, when the animal, having recovered from its operation, is under lengthy observation, the dog is irreplaceable; moreover, it is extremely touching. It is almost a participant in the experiments conducted upon it, greatly facilitating the success of the research by its understanding and compliance."

Hundreds of dogs passed through Pavlov's laboratory, but there is no doubt which was his favorite: a combination of setter and collie that the laboratory named Druzhok (Russian for "Little Friend"). Druzhok earned his name by becoming the first dog to survive an especially important and complex operation: he was given an "isolated small stomach" that, for the first time, allowed Pavlov and his coworkers to study the details of the entire digestive process in the stomach.

Why couldn't they study this process by using a fistula and esophagotomy? If a dog had a gastric fistula and ate

Lab workers take the experimental dogs for a walk on the Institute grounds. One dog is known to have escaped.

some food, a messy mixture of gastric juice and food would come out. It was impossible to separate the food from the juice in order to measure the juice carefully. If a dog had a gastric fistula and an esophagotomy, the food never actually reached the stomach. Such dogs were fine for proving the important role of appetite, but they could not help Pavlov discover what happened when food actually reached the stomach. The isolated stomach allowed Pavlov to study both stages of digestion in the stomach: the first stage, which he had already proved resulted from appetite; and the second stage, which began when food actually reached the stomach.

The isolated stomach operation separated the dog's stomach into a large and a small section. When the dog ate food, it reached the large stomach and stimulated the gastric glands. The small stomach remained connected to the large one by nerves—and so, according to Pavlov, reacted to the food in the exact same way. This small stomach, however, was separated from the large one in a way that prevented food from reaching it. A fistula ran from this small stomach to the outside of the dog's body. When Druzhok ate food, Pavlov could measure the gastric secretions in the small stomach and use this to discover how the large stomach responded to various foods.

For three years, from 1894 through 1897, Pavlov and his coworkers fed Druzhok different kinds of food and collected the gastric juice that flowed after every meal from the dog's isolated sac. They analyzed the amount and strength of the gastric juice after every meal. A single experiment often took 8 or 10 hours—that is, from the time they fed Druzhok until the time the gastric juice stopped dripping out of the fistula. For most of this time, the coworker had to wait patiently, holding a cup under Druzhok in order to catch the drops of gastric juice as they came out of the fistula. It was important to be very still and avoid making any noises while doing this. Noise or movement might excite Druzhok, and this might influence his mood and appetite—

continued on page 56

THE PAVLOV ISOLATED STOMACH

Pavlov used the isolated stomach to investigate the normal digestive processes. He was not the first person to make an isolated sac, but he modified an earlier operation by the German physiologist Rudolf Heidenhain in an important way. To make his isolated sac, Heidenhain had cut the vagal nerves (nerves that run from the brain through the chest and into the stomach), which play an important part in digestion. Therefore, according to Pavlov, Heidenhain's sac distorted the normal digestive process. Pavlov devised a way to create the isolated sac while leaving intact the all-important nervous connections. This made the operation much more difficult, but, in Pavlov's opinion, it was necessary for the creation of a small stomach that responded to food in exactly the same way as did the normal stomach, which was essential to his experiments. This difficult operation became a worldwide symbol of Pavlov's surgical wizardry; many foreign scientists traveled to St. Petersburg in order to learn how to perform it.

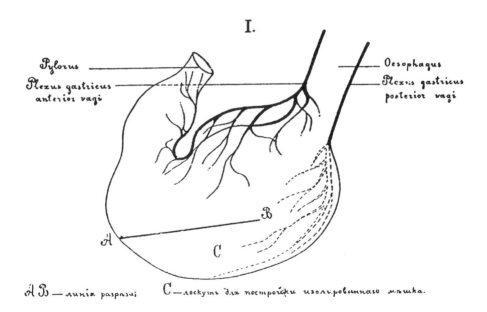

I.

The two diagrams below are reproduced from Pavlov's *Lectures on the Work of the Main Digestive Glands.* Figure 1 shows the dog's stomach before the operation. When the dog eats food, it comes down the esophagus into the stomach (area C). The line AB shows where Pavlov cut the stomach to create the pouch that would become the small stomach. Figure 2 shows the stomach after the operation. Food still comes down the esophagus into the large stomach (area V). The small stomach (area S) is connected by nerves to the large stomach, and so still reacts to the food. Food is prevented from contaminating the small stomach, however, by a layer of mucous (the mucous membrane) between the large and small stomachs.

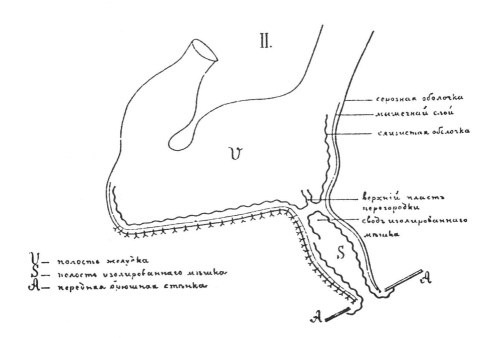

and so change the results of the experiment. Inevitably, disturbances occurred many times—and then Pavlov and his coworkers had to decide whether the change in Druzhok's mood influenced the results of their experiment, and if so, in what way. After Pavlov had reached some basic conclusions from the experiments on Druzhok, he and a coworker checked these with a second dog, Sultan.

We have already seen some of the ingredients in Pavlov's scientific successes: good ideas about an important subject, the ability to devise experiments that would answer key questions, surgical skills, new techniques (including the use of surgically altered animals as tools) and a well-equipped laboratory with coworkers to assist him. If we look closely at his interpretation of experimental results, we will see another important characteristic of great scientists: a good imagination. It is one thing to learn information from a textbook or to conduct an experiment in science class when the teacher has already told you what results you should get. It is quite another to experiment for the first time on something as complicated as the digestive system in a large animal. The results of even the best-conceived experiments will often be messy. Pavlov was very bold about looking at messy results and seeing a pattern.

Let's put ourselves in Pavlov's shoes for a moment, and look at the results of some of the experiments with Druzhok and Sultan. Through his experiments on Druzhok, Pavlov decided that the gastric glands produced a distinctive response to each different food. In other words, when a dog ate 200 grams of meat, the gastric glands produced a specific pattern of secretion; and when it ate 200 grams of bread, the glands produced a different pattern. Pavlov thought that the response to the same amount of the same food should be exactly the same every time. Of course, the results were never exactly the same. Pavlov attributed this fact to changes in the dog's mood and appetite, or to the differences in per-

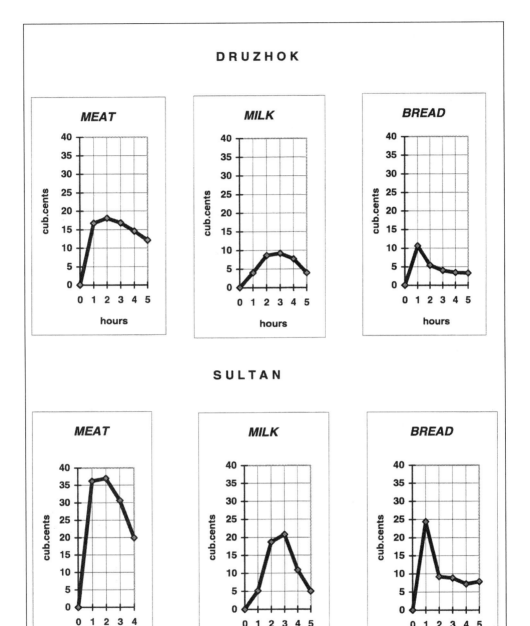

These curves represent the results of Pavlov's experiments on the amount of gastric juice that laboratory dogs Druzhok and Sultan produced when fed meat, milk, or bread.

sonality between two different dogs. But still, he thought he saw an important pattern.

Pavlov converted the results of his experiments into curves. On the horizontal axis he marked the time, and on the vertical axis he recorded the amount of gastric juice. In both dogs, the meat curve reaches its high point in the first or second hour, levels off in the second hour, and then declines slowly; the bread curve reaches its high point in the first hour and then declines quickly; the milk curve reaches its high point in the second or third hour, holds steady for a while, and then declines gradually.

But what about the differences between, say, the meat curves for Druzhok and Sultan? Pavlov thought these curves were basically the same, and that he could explain the minor differences as the result of uncontrolled variables in his experiments. For example, Sultan's meat curve goes much higher than Druzhok's. Pavlov theorized that this could have happened for a number of reasons: perhaps Sultan's stomach was larger, perhaps he liked meat more than did Druzhok (and so produced more "appetite juice"), perhaps Sultan had more fluids in his body than did Druzhok, or perhaps something had excited Sultan during the experiment. Pavlov thought that if he could somehow eliminate these differences between Sultan and Druzhok, the experiments with each dog would have turned out exactly the same.

It is very possible that another scientist might have looked at these curves and decided that the patterns Pavlov saw did not really exist, or that they were not meaningful. This other scientist might, then, have concluded that there was no such thing as a meat curve, a bread curve, and a milk curve. This illustrates an important point about science: It is often possible to draw very different conclusions from the same experimental results. Among other things, science is about imagination and interpretation.

Pavlov's interpretation of his experimental results was related to his basic idea about the digestive system: that it was "a complex chemical factory." The raw material (food) passes along the digestive canal, which is basically just a long tube (like the work area of a large factory). As the food moves down the digestive canal, information goes out to various "workshops" along the way. These workshops were the digestive glands—the salivary glands in the mouth, the gastric glands in the stomach, and the pancreatic gland, which poured its juice onto the food as it was leaving the stomach on its way to the intestines.

According to Pavlov, the information that the digestive canal sent to the digestive glands was just like the orders a factory sent to the small workshops that provided materials for it to make a particular product. In a steel factory, for example, the factory manager ordered specific tools from one workshop, a specific chemical from another, and a second chemical from yet another. Similarly, the digestive canal sent specific orders through special nerves to the digestive glands. These orders said something like: "We have eight ounces of meat, so send us the exact amount and type of digestive juice we need to digest this meal." And, perhaps a few minutes later: "Now we have six ounces of milk on the way. Send the kind of digestive juice that works best on this material." The digestive glands then produced just the right kind of juices and sent them to the digestive canal. There the meat and milk were broken down into a form that could be absorbed into the blood and circulated throughout the animal's body, where it provided nutriment and energy.

text continued on page 62

Pavlov's answer to Snoopy's question would be: The sound stimulates the dog's appetite, which excites the vagus nerve, which causes the gastric glands in the stomach to secrete. In later years, Pavlov would analyze this "appetite juice" as a conditional reflex.

WHY A FACTORY? METAPHORS IN SCIENTIFIC THINKING

I t is interesting that Pavlov came up with his idea that "the digestive system is a complex chemical factory" at the very same time that Russia was undergoing its industrial revolution. In the 1880s and 1890s, about 100 years after this process began in Great Britain, huge factories were springing up throughout Russia, replacing the small workshops that had previously dominated the production of various goods. St. Petersburg became a center of factory production, and the home, for example, of the famous Putilov Iron Works.

Russian intellectuals discussed what this new development signified for Russia's way of life, and the newspapers were full of arguments about whether factory production was a good or bad thing. Some people thought that the appearance of factories meant that the country was acquiring some of the worst features of life in the West, such as an oppressed working class and a preoccupation with money and material things. Others thought that the new factories were a very positive development: they were efficiently producing things that Russia needed, and would strengthen the country's economy and national power.

It is very possible that the emergence of real factories influenced the way Pavlov viewed the digestive system. If this were indeed so, it would be only one of many examples throughout history in which scientists used metaphors drawn from their daily life, or the life of their country, to understand nature.

Nature, after all, is infinitely complicated. Whenever we look at it—and here, too, the scientist is no exception—we must decide which things we see are important and which are meaningless. In a way, it is like looking at the clouds in the sky. If you have birds or baseball stadiums on your mind, you may "see" one of these in the cloud formations. If you have never seen a bird or a baseball stadium, you certainly won't. Many psychologists and philosophers think it is impossible for us to think about anything without using metaphors.

So, for many hundreds of years, great thinkers and explorers of nature thought they saw in it a "great chain of being" in which everything, living and non-living, was arranged in a great chain from highest to lowest. This idea, which was drawn from their culture and their way of life, helped them organize and interpret the things they saw in nature. On the other hand, Charles Darwin, the great 19th-century British naturalist, saw in nature a "struggle for existence," and this concept certainly was influenced by the great social and economic struggles that were part of the everyday life of his country at the time. When great mechanical clocks were hailed as a modern invention, many psychologists thought about the human mind as a clock. Now, when computers are all the rage, many modern scientists think of the brain as a computer.

This does not mean that science is just a matter of opinion—that different people can see nature in different ways and there is no way to tell which way is better. In science, the relationship between image (or theory) and fact is much more complicated than that; and scientists who initially disagree can often come to a common conclusion in the end. They can decide in what ways a specific metaphor is useful and in what way it is not.

The importance of metaphors in scientific thought does, however, remind us that, because scientists are human beings, their ideas are influenced by their own lives and times. Pavlov could not have thought "the brain is a computer" because computers had not been invented yet. And had he lived in a part of Russia that did not have factories or discussions about factories, he would not have been able to think of the digestive system in the way he did.

The digestive machine was especially complicated because it was inhabited by a sort of "ghost"; namely, the animal's psyche—its personality and changing moods, and its food preferences. Remember that earlier, Pavlov and Ekaterina Shumova-Simonovskaia had proved the important role of appetite in making gastric juice flow. If a dog enjoyed eating food, the gastric glands in the stomach began to produce juice even if the food never actually reached the stomach. "Appetite," Pavlov wrote, "is the first and mightiest exciter" of gastric juice in the stomach.

One of Pavlov's first experiments in his new laboratory showed that if an animal was hungry enough, this gastric juice flowed even if the animal merely saw a piece of food. (Some scientists had actually noticed this years before, but they could not make it occur regularly in a laboratory—and so could not convince their colleagues that this was a normal part of digestion.)

This ghost did not act the same way every time. Pavlov noticed that, just like people, different dogs like different foods, and that a dog's food preferences change from day to day and moment to moment. Also like people, dogs have different personalities. Some dogs were "greedier" for food than others, and so they produced more appetite juice. Some dogs were "dreamier" than others: these dogs would be more likely to get their gastric juices flowing just by seeing food. Other dogs were more "cold-blooded": Their gastric glands did not start working until the food was actually in their mouths. Some dogs were "cunning" and easily insulted: If the experimenter showed some food to such a dog without actually feeding it, the dog might think it was being teased and react much as a hungry person would in that situation; that is, it would get angry and turn away from the experimenter rather than producing gastric juice in eager anticipation of a meal.

For these reasons, the personality and mood of a dog added an unpredictable element to the digestive machine. In characterizing his dogs' mood and personality, Pavlov was influenced both by the patterns of gastric flow and by subjective interpretations of the dogs' behavior. The main point is that these experiments did not turn out exactly the same each time. For precisely this reason—that the dogs' psyche did not behave predictably—Pavlov did not think it was a simple reflex.

Another important fact was this: Without "appetite juice," most foods did not get digested. They just remained in the stomach until they rotted. The ghost in the digestive machine—appetite and personality—clearly played a very important role in its function.

Pavlov thought that his experiments explained why some people had problems digesting their food. Too often people ate hurriedly, without paying attention to their food, or they were worried and preoccupied at meals. For this reason, they did not produce the necessary "appetite juice" to digest their food. Although people had not understood this scientifically, they had developed habits and customs to increase their appetite. For example, there was a good scientific basis for having a separate dining room: it divided meals from the business of life, encouraging people to concentrate on their food. Another example was that people everywhere used many spices to make their food tastier—that is, to increase the appetite with which they ate it.

Pavlov summarized the results of his laboratory's research on the digestive system in his book *Lectures on the Work of the Main Digestive Glands* (1897). He analyzed the factorylike operation of the digestive system, explained how the nervous system controlled the entire process, and described the important role played by the animal's psyche. For him, the digestive system was a good example of the perfect adaptation of the animal machine to its environment. It was, he wrote, "an artistic mechanism imbued, like everything in nature, with subtlety and internal purposiveness."

Pavlov emphasized that this conclusion was the result of

The first edition of Pavlov's 1897 book Lectures on the Work of the Main Digestive Glands. *Quickly translated into German, French, and English, this volume brought Pavlov worldwide renown.*

thousands of experiments conducted on hundreds of dogs by scores of coworkers. He gave credit by name to the many coworkers who had actually conducted the experiments in his laboratory. The new picture of the digestive system that he offered was the accomplishment "of the general laboratory atmosphere, which everybody breathed in and to which everybody gave something of himself."

By the year 1900, Pavlov had become very well known to physicians and scientists around the world. The physicians who had worked in his laboratory returned to medical practice and spread the word about Pavlov's research. Scientists from all over the world visited his laboratory in order to learn how to perform the unique surgical operations that Pavlov had perfected. One of Pavlov's coworkers translated his book into German in 1898, and French and English editions appeared within a few years as well. These made Pavlov's discoveries easily accessible to his colleagues in Western Europe and the United States, very few of whom read Russian.

By this time, Pavlov also had come under attack by Russia's anti-vivisectionist movement. The Russian Society for Protection of Animals was but one of a number of groups that emerged in the United States and Europe at the turn of the century with the goal of limiting or ending the use of animals in scientific experiments. The Russian Society labeled vivisection a "cruel and useless abuse" of animals, and its members sometimes attended Pavlov's lectures and published moving accounts of the sad fate of some of his experimental dogs. When the Russian Society insisted in 1903 that only experiments approved by its membership should be permitted, Pavlov and his colleagues at the Military-Medical Academy composed a response that defended the scientific value of animal experiments and argued that a ban on vivisection would, in effect, force physicians to experiment on humans—that is, to test on people medicines that had not yet been tested on laboratory animals. Pavlov added a personal note about his "deep sense of regret" whenever he conducted an experiment that would cost an animal its life. "When I dissect and destroy a living animal, I hear within myself a bitter reproach that, with a rough and blundering hand, I am breaking an inexpressibly artistic mechanism. But I endure this in the interest of truth, for the benefit of humanity."

In 1904, Pavlov became the first physiologist (and the first Russian) to receive the Nobel Prize in physiology or medicine. He and Serafima traveled to Stockholm, Sweden, to receive this great honor from the Swedish king, Oskar II. Out of respect for Pavlov, the king had learned a little Russian, and so was able to surprise him with the greeting: "Kak Vy pozhivaete?" ("How are you?")

Pavlov, too, surprised his audience. The assembled scientists and dignitaries expected him to give a speech about his discoveries concerning the digestive system. Instead, he spoke mostly about his recent investigations of another subject. Pavlov was now studying the "ghost" in the digestive machine—appetite and the psyche. "Only one thing in life really interests us: our psychic life," he explained. Artists, writers, philosophers, and historians had all addressed the nature of human thoughts and emotions. Now it was physiology's turn. For most people in the room, this was the first time they heard the words "conditional reflexes" and "unconditional reflexes"—words that would eventually bring Pavlov even greater renown than had his studies of digestion.

In a letter to Serafima 20 years earlier, Pavlov had written that someday there would be a "science of human life . . . but not soon, not soon." Now, however, he thought that he had found the key to just such a science.

Pavlov in 1904. Having won the Nobel Prize that year for his research on digestion, he had already shifted his attention to conditional reflexes.

Towers of Silence

Pavlov's speech upon accepting the Nobel Prize showed that he had changed his mind about the ghost in the digestive machine. For many years, he had thought that the psyche could not be studied by scientific methods. Science, Pavlov thought, could study only deterministic processes. By "deterministic," he meant processes that obeyed the laws of the physical world and so, in Pavlov's view, were machine-like. That is, they occurred in exactly the same way every time if the circumstances were the same. For example, if you wind up the same watch in exactly the same way 10 times, it will run for exactly the same amount of time (except to the degree that the watch begins to wear out). Similarly, if an experimenter fed the same animal the same amount of the same food 10 times, the stomach would pro-duce the very same amount of gastric juice each time—except when the dog's psyche interfered.

That was precisely the point. The psyche did not seem to work in the same way as a machine worked. It behaved very differently at different times, depending on a dog's mood and personality and taste in food. This was the first reason that, for many years, Pavlov thought the psyche could not be studied scientifically.

The second reason was that it could not be studied objectively. For Pavlov, to be objective was to analyze something using things one could see, smell, or touch—and, better yet, count or measure. Only in this way could a scientist establish the truth about anything. For example, if scientists wanted to know if an iron ball drops through the air at the same speed as a paper ball, they could drop the two balls at the same time and see what happened. If two scientists got two different results, they could compare their experiments to decide who was right.

Nobody, however, can see an animal's thoughts and emotions. Two scientists can watch the same dog do the same thing and have different opinions about what the dog is thinking or feeling. If the experimenter offered the dog a piece of steak and the dog turned its head away, what was the dog thinking or feeling? One person might think the dog was not hungry; another might think the dog did not like meat; and yet another might conclude that the dog thought it was being teased, and so was insulted. For Pavlov, such opinions could never be scientific because they could never be objective. No experiment could settle the question of who was right and who was wrong.

By the time he won the Nobel Prize, however, Pavlov thought that the psyche might well operate in a deterministic manner, and that he had discovered an objective way to study this. He believed he could experiment on the dog's psyche without needing to guess about what the dog was thinking or feeling. In fact, he even began to punish coworkers in his laboratory who mentioned a dog's feelings or thoughts—a habit he now considered unscientific—by fining them a small amount of money.

It had taken Pavlov about six years—as he put it, after "persistant deliberation" and "a difficult intellectual struggle"—to change his mind. He did not do this alone. Some of his coworkers designed new experiments and brought their own ideas to the study of the psyche. Pavlov, however, interpreted the results in his own way to develop a general view and, most important, a new experimental approach to the psyche.

Basically, Pavlov developed a way to use a dog's salivary glands as a window through which to look at its brain. The salivary glands, he had discovered, were especially sensitive to the influence of the psyche. By counting the number of saliva drops that a dog produced in different situations, Pavlov thought he could analyze the complex and invisible processes that turn what an animal sees, smells, hears, and touches into important information about its environment. As with many new ideas, it was easy to make fun of this one. Some of Pavlov's colleagues, who had respected his work on the digestive system, thought this new area of study was a bit bizarre. They joked that he was now work-ing on "spitting science," and even his good friend, the Finnish physiologist Robert Tigerstedt, urged Pavlov to "drop this fad and return to real physiology."

Pavlov himself was both very excited and somewhat fearful. He was excited because he thought that he had found a way to finally make the psyche a subject of scientif-ic investigation. He had been thrilled 40 years earlier by Sechenov's vision about the "reflexes of the brain"—and now he himself was turning this vision into real experimen-tal science. If he succeeded, he might uncover the secrets of human thoughts and emotions, and so might discover what made people love and hate, cooperate and wage war. Per-haps he would even discover how society could produce fewer "bad machines" and more good ones—that is, more generous, intelligent, and noble types of humans. Shortly after his first experiments on this new subject, Pavlov cor-nered some of his colleagues in a hallway and told them excitedly: "Yes, we've got it, look what we've got! You know, there is enough work here for many decades."

He was also, however—as he admitted privately—

constantly "tormented by the beast of doubt." This research was so novel and complicated, and so dependent upon his own interpretations, that he always worried that he might have taken a wrong turn. As one coworker recalled, Pavlov viewed this new research as his "vulnerable child." Even after many years of investigation, his insecurity was obvious in the delight with which he responded to promising experimental results: "Look, this new fact entirely justifies our approach, we could hardly be greatly mistaken."

Another problem for Pavlov was that Serafima disapproved of this new line of research. For her, a deeply religious woman, Pavlov's approach was materialist, and threatened to undermine belief in free will and an immortal soul. While he thought that a scientific understanding of the psyche would allow humans to change themselves and the world for the better, she feared that it would weaken religion and morality. This disagreement about scientific work that lay at the center of Pavlov's very existence undermined the close-

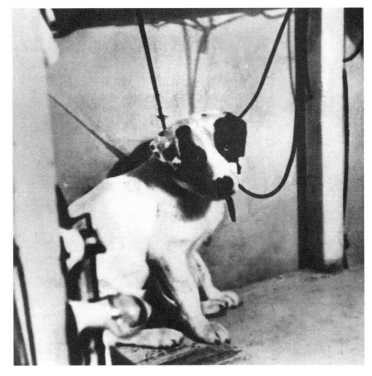

After discovering that salivary glands are highly sensitive to the influence of the psyche, Pavlov designed experiments using a salivary fistula to study the conditional and unconditional reflexes of dogs.

ness of their relationship.

We can understand Pavlov's basic idea by considering two scenarios that are very familiar to anybody who has a pet dog. Scenario 1: A piece of meat is put into the dog's mouth, and the dog salivates. Scenario 2: The person who always feeds the dog walks into the room, and the dog salivates. How can we describe what has happened in each case without guessing what the dog is thinking or feeling? In what ways are the two scenarios the same, and in what ways are they different?

For Pavlov, scenario 1 would be an example of an unconditional reflex. All animals have certain inborn reflexes that serve a particular purpose. The salivary reflex causes the production of saliva when it is necessary to handle a substance in the dog's mouth. If the substance is food, the chemicals in saliva begin digesting it and the liquid washes it down the digestive tract. But if the substance is potentially harmful—such as poison or acid—saliva protects the dog's mouth against damage. In the first scenario, the salivary glands in the dog's mouth respond reflexively to the food. This is an "unconditional" reflex because it does not depend on any conditions—it is an inborn response that occurs the same way every time. The food is an unconditional stimulus, and the salivation is an unconditional response.

For Pavlov, the second scenario would be an example of a conditional reflex. The dog does not have an inborn reflex to salivate upon seeing a person. Why, then, does it salivate upon seeing the particular person that feeds it? Pavlov theorized that this occurs because the person has become a signal for the food. Every time this person fed the dog, the dog had an unconditional reflex to the food, which became linked (or "associated") in the brain with the visual image of the person. The person then became a conditional stimulus, and salivation upon seeing the person became a conditional response. Every conditional reflex, then, is built upon an unconditional reflex. Salivation in the second scenario is a "conditional reflex" because it depends upon certain conditions, and when those conditions change, the reflex also changes. Pavlov and his coworkers discovered, for example, that if the person who usually fed the dog came into the room and did not feed the dog, the next time the dog saw this person it salivated a little less. If the person then reentered the room several more times without feeding the dog, the conditional reflex disappeared entirely. The person ceased to be a signal for the food, and the dog no longer salivated upon seeing him.

The big question for Pavlov was: Do conditional reflexes obey unvarying laws? Are they just more complicated, but no less determined, no less machinelike, than unconditional reflexes? Could he learn how to make them appear and disappear, grow stronger and weaker, and so on, so that they became just as predictable as an unconditional reflex? If so, could he use their laws to study the actual processes in the brain? Pavlov eventually answered all of these questions with an emphatic "yes."

For Pavlov, the existence of unconditional and conditional reflexes explained how an animal survived in and adapted to a changing environment. The animal had a set of unchanging, permanent unconditional reflexes that prepared it for the constant challenges of life: It salivated in response to food, bared its teeth when an enemy approached, and burrowed into the ground to avoid cold weather. On the other hand, an evolving set of conditional reflexes allowed the animal to adapt to its surroundings: to associate a moving bush with a tasty meal, a loud sound with a dangerous enemy, a hump in the earth with a warm place. These conditional reflexes provided information about the environment, and when the environment changed the conditional reflexes changed with them.

For example, assume that for many years a wolf lived in the wild and ate a smaller animal that signaled its presence by making low bushes move. Every time a bush moved, the wolf would associate this—through a conditional reflex— with a possible meal. Now assume that over time this smaller animal died out or migrated to another region. In this case, a moving bush eventually only signaled the blowing of the wind. After checking out a moving bush several times and failing to find the small animal, the wolf's conditional reflex to a moving bush disappears. The temporary nature of conditional reflexes has allowed it to adapt to a changing environment.

The psychic life of animals—their thoughts and emotions—could, then, be approached scientifically as very complex, conditional reflexes. Pavlov believed that the investigation of conditional and unconditional reflexes provided an objective method for uncovering the nature of these processes and the qualities of the brain that produced them. He could now study the complex, invisible processes in the brain in much the same way as he had earlier studied the digestive system: Pavlov and his coworkers conducted thousands of experiments, and Pavlov found in the results

Pavlov (center, seated) and his coworkers with an experimental dog. Just to Pavlov's left is W. Horsley Gantt, the physiologist who later created a Pavlovian laboratory at the Johns Hopkins University in Baltimore.

certain basic patterns in dogs' salivary responses to various situations.

He eventually decided that he could explain these patterns as basically the result of three things: First, every environmental stimulus led to one of the two basic nervous processes: excitation or inhibition. Pavlov often compared the nervous system to the Roman god Janus, with its two faces looking in opposite directions. One face, excitation, was the process by which a stimulus (such as a sight, smell, or sound) caused a nervous impulse to move a body part. The other face, inhibition, was the process by which a stimulus led to a nervous impulse that blocked the movement of a body part. The relative strength of excitation and inhibition was constantly changing, and this "balance of power" governed the animal's behavior. Second, the nervous processes of excitation and inhibition spread and interacted in the brain according to certain basic laws. Third, there were inborn differences between the nervous systems of different individuals. In some individuals, the nervous system tended to favor excitation; in others, it tended to favor inhibition. These inborn differences explained why different dogs responded differently to identical experiments. Pavlov thought that people also had inborn variations in their nervous systems—in the balance between excitation and inhibition—and that this partially explained why two people responded differently to the same situation.

We can appreciate the power and novelty of Pavlov's approach to the psyche by considering one very difficult question that he attempted to answer: How acute is a dog's sense of time? Can a dog sense the difference between a minute and an hour, or between 5 seconds and 10 seconds? If you imagine yourself trying to answer this question by simply observing a dog and trying to guess what it is thinking or feeling, you will see how difficult that would be. Pavlov and his coworkers, however, used the conditional reflexes method to study this in great detail. First, they put a hungry dog in a room with a metronome that beat at a certain speed—say, 60 beats per minute. At the end of that minute, they fed the dog. They repeated this procedure several times to establish a conditional reflex. Now, every time the metronome beat, the dog salivated. (The metronome has become a conditional stimulus, and salivation the conditional response.)

Pavlov and his coworkers then experimented to see what happened when they changed the speed of the metronome and did not feed the dog. For example, they slowed the metronome to 40 beats per minute, and at the end of that time they did not feed the dog. They then sped the metronome back up to 60 beats per minute and did feed the dog. They repeated this procedure with 40 and 60 beats per minute several times. They discovered that, in the first few experiments, the dog salivated at the end of a 40-beat minute. Thus far, it had formed a conditional reflex to the beating of the metronome itself—and not to the beating of the metronome at a certain speed. After a number of repetitions, however, the dog did not salivate when the metronome beat 40 times per minute. It did, however, salivate when the metronome beat 60 times per minute.

This response demonstrated what Pavlov called the process of differentiation: the beating of the metronome excited a salivary response, but that response was now inhibited when the metronome beat 40 times per minute. The experiment demonstrated that a dog's sensory organs can distinguish between these two time intervals. By conducting experiments with increasingly smaller differences (say, with 58 and 60 beats of the metronome per minute), Pavlov and his coworkers discovered how sensitive a dog was to the passing of time. Similar experiments established a dog's ability to distinguish between different shades of light, and between a circle and various kinds of ellipses.

According to Pavlov, this process of differentiation was the means by which all animals (including humans) develop through experience a subtle understanding of the world around them. For example, we might get excited whenever a car pulls up in front of our home; but over time we form an association between a specific car—a white one with a dent on the front fender—and Mom or Dad's arrival home from work. The specificity of this association results from the interplay of excitation (the response of our nervous system to the arrival of any car) and inhibition (the blocking of this response for all cars other than the white one with a dent on the front fender).

For this reason, Pavlov thought that the very existence of complex animals depended upon the dynamic relationship of "these two halves—of excitation and inhibition. . . . The external world perpetually elicits, on the one hand, conditional reflexes, and, on the other hand, continually suppresses them" through inhibition. Pavlov concluded that it was through this process that an animal "responds at any given moment to the demand of the fundamental law of life—a balance with surrounding nature."

Some animals did so better than others. Pavlov noticed that different dogs responded in various ways to the same experiments. For example, one dog might differentiate between the two speeds of the metronome very quickly—after just one or two repetitions—while another dog consistently failed to do so. Pavlov concluded that dogs were born with different types of nervous systems, and therefore, with what we might call different "personalities." The strength of excitation and inhibition in the nervous systems of some dogs was wonderfully balanced, but in other dogs, there was an imbalance. Some dogs were easily excited and had weak inhibition; others were just the opposite. Dogs with both types of unbalanced nervous system were much slower to differentiate among various stimuli, and thus adapted to their environment less well than did those with well-balanced systems. Pavlov concluded that the same thing was true for people.

Just as a balance between excitation and inhibition was necessary for an animal to gain a correct and subtle understanding of its environment, so a balance between freedom and discipline was necessary to a properly functioning person, society, and culture. People who were too excitable or too inhibited could not possibly understand reality correctly and respond to it reasonably. Similarly, Pavlov thought that the nervous systems of certain "national types" (the Germans and the English, for instance) were superbly balanced, enabling them to make especially outstanding contributions to science, literature, and industry. He worried that Russians often had an imbalanced nervous system, and that this deficiency was partially responsible for his country's slow social progress. He also believed, however, that his laboratory experiments showed that weak, imbalanced nervous systems could be improved by the proper training and environment. In fact, later in his life Pavlov launched a scientific project designed to improve the nervous system of humans.

To study conditional reflexes, Pavlov designed an entirely new type of laboratory, which became known as the "Towers of Silence." He had discovered that his dogs' conditional reflexes were affected by even very subtle changes—by a small rise in the temperature of the air or the faint vibrations of a passing carriage. For his experiments to be absolutely precise, he needed, then, to have complete control over even such small details. The "Towers of Silence," then, were just that: a place where dogs would be absolutely isolated from everything except the stimulus that Pavlov was testing. The building had thick concrete walls and was surrounded by a moat; the rooms in which experiments were conducted floated on a layer of water to muffle any outside vibrations. When conducting experiments, Pavlov and his coworkers did not even enter the room: Special machines allowed them to feed the dog, shine a light, or start a metronome beating while observing and measuring the saliva drops from outside.

The Towers of Silence: Its thick walls and insulated floors were designed to give Pavlov control over even small details of the environment of his experimental dogs.

As he pursued this research in the early 1900s, Pavlov flourished as never before. The Nobel Prize had brought him material comfort and worldwide fame. He was elected to scientific societies throughout the world, and in 1907 he became a member of Russia's exalted Academy of Sciences. He now ran three separate laboratories, and a growing number of scientists traveled to St. Petersburg from Germany, France, Great Britain, and the United States in order to work with him and study his scientific methods. His four children, too, were prospering—Vsevolod had become a jurist, Vladimir a physicist, and Viktor a promising science student; Vera worked alongside her father, conducting research on conditional reflexes.

Whether inside or outside his laboratory, Pavlov lived by an unvarying schedule. From September to early May he worked constantly, walking briskly through St. Petersburg among his three laboratories. On Friday evenings, at precisely 7:00, a group of friends came to his apartment to play cards. Pavlov so loved punctuality and precision that, if his friends arrived even one minute early, they would wait in the corridor in order to knock on his door at just the right moment. Pavlov spent his summers at his dacha (a summer home in the country), where he gardened, swam, bicycled, and read novels. Even when he was relaxing, he insisted on physical exercise every day, to experience what he called "muscular joy."

By 1914, then, Pavlov was on top of the world. At age 65, he was a financially secure and world-renowned scientist; busier than ever, he thought he might be on the road to discovering the key to human emotions and behavior. He could not have known that his entire world was about to be turned upside down, and that a new and dramatic chapter in his life was about to unfold.

CHAPTER 5

After the Revolution

In August 1914 Pavlov's world began crashing down around him. World War I sounded the death knell for tsarist Russia. Tsar Nicholas II's huge empire proved too poor, too weak, and too politically divided to wage a long war. At one point, many Russian soldiers were sent to the front without weapons—they were told to pick them up from their fellow soldiers as they were killed. By the end of the war in 1918, more than 1.5 million Russian soldiers had died in the slaughter; another 4 million were wounded or taken prisoner by the advancing German armies.

Cold, hungry, and demoralized, the Russian army began to disintegrate as soldiers deserted and straggled home. There the situation was increasingly desperate. There was not enough fuel to keep factories and even bakeries going, and workers in the cities left their jobs to search for food in the countryside.

On top of all this, Nicholas II and his wife, Alexandra, were increasingly mistrusted by the population—even by the nobles and government leaders who surrounded them. Alexandra had fallen under the influence of a mysterious peasant from Siberia named Rasputin. Rasputin had gained

Red Army soldiers in December 1920 with skis and a machine gun mounted on a sled. The bloody civil war between the Reds and Whites lasted from 1918 to 1921.

her confidence by his ability—probably through hypnosis—to stop the bleeding of her hemophiliac son Alexei. Convinced that only Rasputin could save their son's life, the royal couple clung to him despite his outrageous and sinister behavior. For many, it was as if an evil spell had descended on the tsar's Winter Palace.

In February 1917 a mass uprising of the Russian people overthrew Nicholas II and the tsarist system, bringing to power a new government that promised Western-style freedoms. That government, however, lasted only about eight months. In October 1917 the Bolshevik party, under the leadership of Vladimir Lenin, seized power.

Lenin and his party promised the long-suffering people "Peace, Land, and Bread." That is, they promised to end the war, to distribute the vast lands of rich landowners to the peasants, and to provide a good life for ordinary workers and peasants under a new social system: socialism. As Lenin explained it, under socialism, Russia's land, mineral resources, and factories would no longer belong to the rich, but rather to the state, which would use them, not for the profits of the few, but for the prosperity of the great majority. On October 25, 1917, the Bolshevik party seized control of the Winter Palace and other key government buildings in St. Petersburg and Moscow. "We shall now proceed to the building of socialism," Lenin proclaimed.

Seizing power proved easier than keeping it. A civil war erupted between the Bolsheviks' Red Army and their opponents' White Army. The Bolsheviks signed a peace treaty with the Germans in 1917, ending Russia's participation in World War I, but the country's civil war continued for more than two years. By the middle of 1921, after a bloody seesaw battle, the Red Army had triumphed and Bolshevik control over the country was complete.

Russia was terribly devastated. Some 20 million people

An idealized portrait of Lenin's return to Russia from exile in April 1917. He led the Bolshevik seizure of power six months later and ruled until his death in 1924.

had died during these years in World War I and the civil war, as well as from famine and typhus epidemics. The country's industry and agriculture lay in ruins, and many of its best-educated people had fled the country.

For Pavlov, these were the darkest of times. Although he had criticized the tsar, he despised the Bolsheviks, whom he considered bloody tyrants who would ruin his country with their unrealistic theories. During the civil war, when food and fuel grew scarce, he watched helplessly as some of his fellow scientists died of cold and hunger. The Bolsheviks confiscated Pavlov's Nobel Prize money, and he was forced, at age 70, to scavenge for firewood and to grow food for his family in a garden that he tended near one of his laboratories. (This task was especially difficult since he had acquired a permanent limp from a fall a few years earlier.) One of Pavlov's sons, Vsevelod, joined the White Army, and when the Red Army won, Vsevolod was forced to emigrate. (He was able to return eight years later.) Another son, Viktor, died during a typhus epidemic. When the Bolsheviks cracked down on their political opponents from 1918 to 1920, Pavlov's home was searched repeatedly, and he and his oldest son, Vladimir, were briefly arrested.

Pavlov also found it impossible to continue his beloved scientific work. His coworkers left for the front, his dogs died of starvation, and, as he wrote to a colleague in 1918, "Work has almost completely ceased. There are no candles, no kerosene, and electricity is provided for only a limited number of hours. Bad, very bad. When will there be a turn for the better?"

By June 1920 Pavlov was desperate, and he wrote a letter to the Bolshevik government explaining that he wanted to emigrate. "I have not much longer to live," he wrote. "I have entered my eighth decade, but my brain still works properly and I very much want to more or less complete my work of many years" on conditional reflexes. This, he explained, was now impossible—indeed, life itself had become virtually impossible: "My wife and I eat very poorly, in both amount and quality; for years we have not seen white bread, for weeks and months at a time we have no milk or meat, feeding largely upon black bread of poor quality, which naturally is causing us gradually to waste away and lose our strength." Pavlov also told the Bolshevik leadership frankly that he was "profoundly convinced" that their policies would lead to the "death of my homeland."

Lenin read Pavlov's letter and decided that Russia could not afford to let such an important scientist leave the country. He also decided that the Bolsheviks should provide everything Pavlov needed to live comfortably and work successfully—to give him, as Serafima later put it, "everything that he wants." At Lenin's instructions, the government issued a special decree that formed a committee responsible for creating the "very best conditions" for Pavlov's life and work.

At the same time as the Bolshevik government was giving Pavlov this "blank check," scientists in the West discouraged him from emigrating. He was, after all, more than 70 years old, and they thought that his best days were behind him. They could not promise Pavlov what he needed to continue his scientific work abroad—only in Russia could he have had a large laboratory with many coworkers. Pavlov loved his homeland and had always been sad about the idea of leaving. Now he decided to stay. Lenin's government was soon showering him with everything he needed for his scientific work, supporting Pavlov much more generously than the tsarist state ever had.

The endless flow of money did not, however, buy his silence. Even as the Bolsheviks suppressed other voices of opposition, Pavlov criticized them loudly and bitterly. "We live under the rule of the cruel principle that the state is everything and that the person is nothing," he said in a speech in 1929. "Naturally, this transforms citizens into a quivering, slavish mass." By 1929 Lenin had died and been replaced by Joseph Stalin, a tyrannical, bloody dictator.

From his boyhood days, when he assisted his father in the family's fruit orchard, Pavlov was an avid gardener.

Stalin's Communist party (the new name for the Bolsheviks) attempted to control all aspects of life, demanding that art, literature, film, and even science be brought into line with their own views. Millions of people were arrested—many for their political views, and many simply because there had been some suggestion that they might be disloyal to Stalin. Pavlov denounced this terror and used his influence to save some of his coworkers from the growing prison camps. Although he considered religion to be incompatible with true science, he denounced the Communists' persecution of religion and threw a big Christmas party every year to make his point.

As the Communist state continued to shower money on Pavlov, his laboratories swung into high gear. He wrote to one colleague in 1923 that "My work is developing on a broad scale. I have many workers and cannot even accept everybody who wants to work here." With expanded modern facilities, numerous coworkers, and endless funds, Pavlov studied many different aspects of what we might call thinking and emotions in animals. Pavlov used a term that he considered more objective and scientific: the "physiology of higher nervous activity"—that is, the physiology of the brain.

Pavlov's basic goals always remained the same: to understand scientifically everything a dog might do in every experimental situation, to understand how the brain worked to produce thoughts, emotions, and behaviors; and to use this scientific knowledge to improve medicine and to understand—and perhaps eventually to change—human behavior.

Among the interesting questions Pavlov studied were

these: How do the conditional reflexes of various animals (for example, fish, mice, dogs, and chimpanzees) compare with each other? What are the different personalities (or "nervous types," as Pavlov called them) of dogs? Are conditional reflexes and personality differences inherited? That is, if a mouse is trained to run through a maze quickly, will its offspring run through the same maze more quickly than those of an "uneducated" mouse? (Pavlov at first thought he had proved that they did—and announced this discovery with great pride—but was later convinced that these experiments were flawed and proved nothing at all.) Pavlov's laboratory also studied the nature of sleep, dreams, and mental illness.

As in earlier years, Pavlov ran his laboratories like small factories, telling his coworkers precisely what to investigate and how. Or, as a coworker of these years put it, his laboratory represented "the life of a single powerful organism, the soul and brain of which was a single brilliant man—Ivan Pavlov." Unlike earlier years, many of Pavlov's coworkers were young professors who taught at other institutions. These professors sometimes developed their own ideas about research, which created problems because Pavlov insisted upon making all important decisions in the laboratory. A number of these coworkers were also supporters of the Bolshevik government, and argued with Pavlov about politics. Pavlov, however, judged his coworkers as scientists and scientists only, praising the achievements of even the most outspoken Communists. Good relations were strained, however, when coworkers wanted to follow a different direction. For example, when one coworker—whom Pavlov had come to regard almost as a son—suggested a new approach to one complicated scientific problem, Pavlov responded: "This is nonsense. Take the usual path, it is more reliable." When the coworker insisted, he finally allowed him to do things his own way—but pointedly ignored him and his work for two entire years.

Before 1917 very few Russian women had become

In 1923, Pavlov collected his articles and speeches about conditional reflexes into a volume entitled Twenty Years of Experience in the Objective Study of the Higher Nervous Activity of Animals. *Translated rapidly into various languages, it provided most scientists with their first exposure to this research.*

scientists, but the Communist government encouraged women to do so, and a number of them found their way to Pavlov's laboratory. One of these women was Rita Rait-Kovaleva, a talented writer and translator with an interest in psychology. Rait-Kovaleva described the atmosphere of "exalted and pure scientific thinking" that surrounded Pavlov, and recalled that she, like other coworkers, learned to think more precisely by practicing exactly what they would say when their demanding chief came to see their experiments. In the 1920s, Rait-Kovaleva was a firm supporter of the Bolshevik government and was surprised by Pavlov's constant criticisms of it. When Pavlov returned from a visit to France in the late 1920s, she heard him say something that signaled a slight change in his attitude: Pavlov told her that he had been stunned by the poor scientific facilities of his French colleagues, who usually worked without adequate space, modern equipment, or the necessary experimental animals. After a moment's silence—during which he thought about his own good fortune—he added: "Yes, you must give our barbarians their due: They understand the value of science."

Pavlov continued to denounce the government for its arrests of masses of innocent people, its persecution of religion, and its failure to provide a decent life for the Russian people. Yet he also increasingly praised it for its great support for science. From his days as a youth in the seminary, Pavlov had always believed that science was the most powerful source of human progress. As a mature man in his 80s, he was more than ever convinced that this was true. Science, he wrote, was "the greatest and fundamental strength of mankind." Scientific progress would not only make humankind the master of nature's limitless wealth, but it would also teach people how to think properly and therefore live together more humanely.

Accidents often prove important in science, and Rita Rait-Kovaleva witnessed an important accident that pushed

Pavlov's investigations in a new direction: On a windy September day in 1924, the Neva River, which flows through the center of St. Petersburg (now called Leningrad), overflowed its banks. The rising water flooded bridges and streets, toppled telephone poles, submerged trolley tracks, and cut off the city's electricity. One of Pavlov's laboratories was located just across the street from the Neva, and Rait-Kovaleva and other coworkers realized that the dogs would be trapped in their cages and drowned. A group of coworkers hurried to the lab, where they found the dogs swimming for their lives at the very tops of their cages, which had been filled almost completely by the rising water.

The doors to the cages were already submerged in water, so in order to save the dogs the coworkers had to grab them and drag them underwater. We might say (although Pavlov doubtless would not approve) that the terrified animals "thought" the coworkers were drowning them, and resisted with all their might. Most of the dogs were saved and moved to safety on the second floor of the lab. The waters began to recede, the laboratory was cleaned up, and experiments continued.

Rait-Kovaleva's dog swiftly recovered and returned "to work." Not so the dogs of two other coworkers, Aleksei Speranskii and Viktor Rikman. Their dogs' previously reliable conditional reflexes had changed or disappeared. (For example, a dog that had been trained to salivate at the sound of a metronome no longer did so.) After about two weeks, Pavlov and his coworkers became convinced that these dogs' strange behavior had resulted from their experiences during the flood. They set up a "decisive experiment" to find out: Harnessing Speranskii's dog to its stand, they created a small flood in the laboratory with a fire hose. "It is difficult to write about what occurred with this poor pup," Rait-Kovaleva later recalled. "It tossed about on its paws, whimpered, tried to tear away from the stand! And after this it didn't eat, gave no reflexes, and, in a word, was 'broken.'"

This discovery was the beginning of the laboratory's exploration of "experimental neurosis." Why did some dogs recover from the flood, while others were permanently affected? What were the nervous processes that led to such "nervous illnesses"? Were these experimental findings applicable to humans, and to the treatment of mental illness? Pavlov and his coworkers addressed these questions throughout the years after the Leningrad flood, and Pavlov himself began regularly to visit a psychiatric clinic, and even to diagnose patients.

In 1929, the 80-year-old Pavlov received a special birthday present from the government: his own scientific village in Koltushi, which was located in the countryside just outside Leningrad. (By this age, the great majority of scientists were well into their retirement years, but Pavlov was as energetic and passionate about his work as ever.) The Koltushi complex was built to Pavlov's specifications, at great expense and very rapidly. Why the hurry? The aging Pavlov stressed that fulfilling the "exceptionally important task" of the Koltushi complex required "my personal participation," and clearly his own time was limited. As he wrote to one of the leaders of the Soviet government, Viacheslav Molotov,

"I have the greatest desire, to the extent that my strength permits, to place this matter on a firm and fruitful basis for the use and glory, most of all, of my homeland."

What was this important task? As Pavlov explained: "Our work will result in the success of eugenics—the science of the development of an improved human type." The word "eugenics" (from Greek words meaning "well" and "born") had been coined by English scientist Francis Galton more than 50 years earlier as a name for a new science devoted to the biological improvement of human beings. Galton and many other scientists were convinced that many physical, moral, and mental traits were inherited. Scientists and governments, they reasoned, should work together to encourage people with desirable traits to have more children, and to discourage (or prevent) those with undesirable traits from having offspring. In this way, the biological stock of the human race would be gradually improved—just as breeders had used this method of selective breeding to develop cows that produced more milk and horses that galloped more quickly.

Of course, people in different countries had widely varying ideas about what traits were desirable in people, and

Pavlov's science village in Koltushi. The Communist state celebrated Pavlov's 80th and 85th birthdays with massive funding for this new facility, which was named The Institute of Experimental Genetics of Higher Nervous Activity.

how to choose those who should breed more and those who should breed less. Class and racial prejudices often played a big role in these choices. The very idea of such a "science" was quite controversial. Still, many leading scientists saw eugenics as a modern way to put science at the service of human progress. One of the early leaders of the Russian eugenics movement was a friend of Pavlov's, the geneticist Nikolai Kol'tsov. For Kol'tsov, the "high ideal" of eugenics was "the creation, through conscious work by many generations, of a higher type of human being, a powerful ruler of nature and creator of life."

Pavlov thought that his laboratory research could provide the scientific basis for a eugenics that would produce this "higher type" with "the most perfected nervous system." His goal was to discover to what degree the strengths and weaknesses of these nervous types were inherited and to what degree they could be changed by controlling environment. He needed, then, to discover the hereditary and environmental conditions that would produce dogs (and, later, people) with the ideal balance of excitation and inhibition. According to Pavlov, such people would make better life decisions and more scientific discoveries—and they would be more likely to survive life's stresses. (Just as some dogs had recovered after the Leningrad flood of 1924, others—who Pavlov thought were a weaker "nervous type"—had been "broken" by the experience.)

This research, Pavlov believed, could only be pursued in an isolated scientific village like Koltushi, where the life conditions of his experimental dogs could be completely controlled. Koltushi would become an enormous "Tower of Silence" in which dogs spent their entire lives, from birth to death—with their every experience controlled and monitored by scientists. Scientists would then study the offspring of these dogs and determine how heredity and life experience influenced the nervous qualities of that next generation. Unlike previous research on conditional reflexes, experiments of this type necessarily took years to complete, since dogs breed relatively slowly. Scientists working with fruit flies or mice can observe numerous new generations in the course of a few months. A dog, however, can produce no more than one new generation in that time. Therefore, Pavlov had no choice but to wait—however impatiently—for the results of this experiment.

He was constantly delighted, however, by his experiences with another area of research at Koltushi: his studies of the mental abilities of two apes named Roza and Rafael. For many years, Pavlov and his coworkers had been interested in comparing their results with dogs to those with other animals. Pavlov spent many hours observing Roza and Rafael and testing their ability to solve various problems (for example, stacking boxes in a pile to stand on in order to obtain food that hung beyond their reach). Unlike experimental dogs, Roza and Rafael were not harnessed to a stand—indeed, they often roamed freely around Koltushi. One of Pavlov's granddaughters later recalled that Roza once wandered into their home while they were eating breakfast. The children were frightened, for they had learned through bitter experience that the apes were not

Rafael demonstrates his puzzle-solving abilities during an experiment at Koltushi.

always the gentlest of playmates. Pavlov, however, laughed and warned his granddaughters that he was comparing these animals' every reaction to their own.

Indeed, Roza's and Rafael's behavior so closely resembled that of humans that it was often difficult to describe in the objective language that Pavlov demanded, excluding references to thoughts and feelings. Pavlov himself once called Rafael "a fool" because of the many mistakes he committed in

Pavlov was a fierce competitor at gorodki, *a traditional Russian game in which players throw heavy wooden pins at other pins arranged in various formations.*

one experiment. "What a muddle he has in his head!" he exclaimed. On the whole, however, Pavlov was very impressed with the mental abilities of these primates, and this led him to modify some of his earlier theories in favor of a more complex conception of mental processes in higher animals.

Koltushi became known as the "World Capital of Conditional Reflexes" and attracted many foreign visitors. It also became Pavlov's favorite place to live and relax. As the years passed, he spent more and more of his time there, with family members coming to stay intermittently, often in the summers. He enjoyed walking and bicycling in the Russian countryside, gardening, and playing his beloved *gorodki*. Pavlov's coworkers were regularly rounded up into teams to play this game, and their forceful and competitive chief berated them at great length when they missed a throw. Pavlov especially loved to pass the time in the glassed-in, second-floor porch of his home there.

It was there, in Pavlov's Koltushi home, that the Russian artist Mikhail Nesterov painted his portrait of the aging scientist, in which he sought to capture the qualities of this "extraordinary man, who was as distinctive and direct as a person can be." Nesterov left this description of a few hours in the life of his lively subject:

> At precisely seven o'clock in the morning I heard Ivan Petrovich leave his study for the stairs. Limping, he

descended the wooden steps and went to swim. He swam every day. . . . Neither rain nor wind would stop him. Quickly undressing, he entered the water, plunged underwater a few times, and quickly redressed. Very rapidly he returned home—where we already awaited him at the breakfast table—greeted us, and had his tea. Over tea the conversations were usually enlivened by Ivan Petrovich himself, who would give improvised, brilliant lectures on any subject. Nothing was foreign to Pavlov's bright intellect. He could speak about biology or other scientific subjects, or about literature and life. He always spoke clearly, imaginatively, convincingly.

Nesterov detected a basic honesty and integrity in the famous scientist: "When Pavlov didn't understand something, he simply admitted it without any false pride," and he spoke to everybody—whether a coworker or a high government official—in the same manner. "He was in everything a distinctive man."

Mikhail Nesterov's painting of Pavlov on the veranda of his home at Koltushi. The artist sought to capture the scientist's passion as expressed in his characteristic gesture of striking his fists against the table when making a point in conversation.

Pavlov addresses the 15th International Congress of Physiologists in 1935.

CHAPTER 6

"The Prince of World Physiology"

If human lives have a climax, it is only fitting that Ivan Pavlov's exceptionally long and rich life had two. The first came in 1904, when, at age 55, his research on the digestive system culminated in winning the Nobel Prize. The second came in 1935, when, at age 85, he hosted the 15th International Congress of Physiologists.

The Congress embodied Pavlov's deep belief in the international community of science and his fervent desire that his country play an honored role in it. Pavlov had invited his colleagues to hold this event in his homeland, and his great prestige overcame the misgivings that many people had about holding it in Stalin's Soviet Union. For the Congress, 900 physiologists from 37 different countries arrived in Leningrad, where they were joined by 500 Russian scientists. The Communist government spared no expense to welcome and impress these delegates: The city's streets were thoroughly cleaned and hung with bright banners, scientific institutions were repainted and freshly equipped, huge banquets for the visiting scientists were held in the beautiful palaces of Russia's former princes, and the entire Congress was transported hundreds of miles from Leningrad to Moscow for the climactic banquet in the very center of state power, the Kremlin.

The international flavor of the Congress was captured in a speech by the eminent Scottish physiologist George Barger. Barger began his speech in English, and then switched successively to French, German, Italian, Swedish, Spanish, and finally Russian. (Pavlov, who spoke foreign languages poorly and with great difficulty, was amazed: "There is another language, and yet another, and yet another!" he exclaimed. "How does one person do such a thing?") In an expression of great respect, Barger pronounced Pavlov the "Prince of World Physiology," eliciting thunderous applause from the audience.

Deeply moved by the Congress, Pavlov expressed his gratitude to the Communist government—which he had criticized so fiercely—for its generous support of Russian science. He added: "As you know, I am an experimenter from head to toe," and expressed his hope that the government's "experiment" with socialism would prove successful. He even proposed a toast to "the great social experimenters." Even as he praised the government's achievements, however, Pavlov did what he could for the victims of its crimes: For example, a woman who cleaned the dogs' cages at one of Pavlov's labs was freed from prison only because Pavlov insisted that her work was important to the success of the Congress; and even at the Congress itself, Pavlov used a spare moment to talk to a Communist leader and win the release of one of his coworkers. This was a time of mass arrests for the flimsiest of political reasons, many of which are still unknown today, buried in secret police archives.

After the Congress, Pavlov resumed his usual 16-hour workdays, walking briskly through Leningrad between his laboratories and the psychiatric clinic where he studied patients and discussed his coworkers' research. He spent his weekends and what turned out to be the last summer of his life combining work and pleasure at Koltushi. Pavlov maintained his brisk schedule even though a near-fatal bout with pneumonia just before the Congress had seriously undermined his health. Longtime coworker Vladimir Savich, noting that by working through the summer Pavlov was departing from his usual routine, thought that Pavlov perhaps had a premonition of approaching death and so wanted to use every remaining moment to pursue his scientific projects.

After a second attack of pneumonia, the 86-year-old scientist died on February 27, 1936. Like Charles Darwin and Louis Pasteur before him, he was eulogized both as a national hero and a leader of international science. Tens of thousands of Leningraders lined the black-draped streets to greet the funeral procession as it proceeded through the city. The Soviet Union's scientific institutions held mass meetings to recognize the great scientist's services. Condolences poured into the country from all over the world.

This great outpouring of respect reflected Pavlov's stature, not only as a scientist, but as an important figure in 20th-century culture. Even today, many people throughout the world who know little or nothing about physiology recall Pavlov and his salivating dogs when they hop to their feet at the sound of the telephone ringing. Like Charles Darwin and Sigmund Freud, Pavlov contributed, not only specific discoveries, but also a sweeping scientific vision—and that vision, and the continuing controversies that surround it, has became part of our never-ending quest to understand the meaning of being human.

Science has changed much since Pavlov's time. Researchers are much more likely today to use sophisticated technologies to study cellular and subcellular mechanisms than they are to work in the Pavlovian style with intact and "normal" animals. In many countries—including the United States—restrictions on the use of animals in experi-

Each panel of the Institute of Experimental Medicine's monument to the dog bears a quotation by Pavlov. The panel on the far left says, in Russian, "Let the dog, man's helper and friend since prehistoric times, offer itself as a sacrifice to science. But our moral dignity obligates us to ensure that this always occurs without unnecessary pain."

ments discourage scientists from conducting the type of research that Pavlov favored. Scientists who study the intact, normal animal often rely upon imaging technologies rather than upon vivisection. For all these reasons, few scientists today are masters of the surgical techniques that Pavlov employed. The explanatory models found in today's scientific texts about digestion and the brain usually differ considerably from Pavlov's.

Pavlov's legacy to science, however, continues to be quite substantial. One indication of this in the United States is the still-vigorous Pavlovian Society, which was founded in 1955 by scientists with a common interest in Pavlov's techniques and insights. The society's regular meetings bring together scientists from various disciplines who use methods and perspectives originating with Pavlov to study such varied subjects as memory, stress, drug addiction, the heart and blood pressure, digestion, the aging process, and the formation of personality.

Scientists who study digestion today rarely use Pavlov's metaphor of the digestive system as a complex chemical factory, but they do accept his basic argument that the digestive system responds sensitively to varied stimuli. They also agree that psychological factors and the nervous system play an important role in digestion. In fact, it turns out that the greatest concentration of nerves in our body—second only to the brain—is in the stomach. This fact has led some scientists to refer (metaphorically) to the "gut-brain." Even in Pavlov's day, however, a third important factor in digestion was discovered: endocrines (internal bodily secretions that regulate physiological processes). Digestive physiologists today often refer to the "psycho-neuro-endocrinological complex" that controls digestion—that is, to the interplay of psychological factors, nerves, and endocrines. Pavlov's insistence on the importance of nerves turns out—as so consistently occurs in science—to be but one part of a more complex reality.

The sciences of the brain and behavior have been revolutionized in the 20th century—and no single approach or model holds a monopoly. For that reason, scientists in these fields today hold varying opinions about Pavlov's ideas. There is no denying, however, the continued importance of Pavlov's legacy here as well. Recently, science writer Dolores Kong interviewed a number of scientists in the United States who draw upon Pavlov's basic ideas and methods in their research. Karen Hollis, a professor of psychology at Mount Holyoke College, noted that, for her, the "critical piece of information" that Pavlov provided was that psychological processes profoundly affect the physiological working of the body—whether or not we are aware of it. So, for example, your responses to a particular place, smell, voice, or face (even your dislike of spinach) may be the results of a conditional reflex formed by an early experience that you may not even remember—but your body does. Neurophysiologists, psychologists, and psychiatrists have been uncovering the role of conditional reflexes in drug addiction, the regulation of blood pressure and body temperature, and the operation of the immune system.

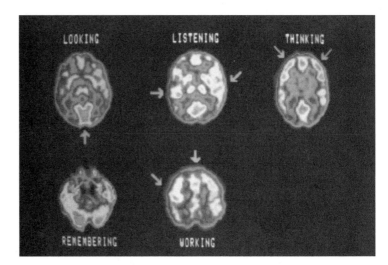

Positron emission tomography (a PET scan) allows scientists today to watch the nervous responses of the brain during the performance of various tasks. The shaded areas represent different levels of metabolic activity.

These discoveries may well prove significant for the treatment of various health problems in the future.

As a pioneering scientist in these fields, Pavlov would have taken great pride in these developments. Nor would he have been surprised that some of the ideas that he defended so vigorously have been discarded. That, as he knew well, is the very nature of science. Toward the end of Pavlov's life, one coworker, in a moment of enthusiasm, predicted that soon they would know everything about the brain. Pavlov turned upon him fiercely: "The more we discover, the more the unknown will reveal itself and the more questions will arise," he insisted. "The path to knowledge is endless."

1849

Ivan Petrovich Pavlov born in Ryazan, Russia, on September 26

1869

Graduates from Ryazan Theological Seminary

1870–75

Attends St. Petersburg University

1876–80

Studies medicine at Military-Medical Academy

1880–83

Marries Serafima Vasil'evna Karchevskaia; begins research on the nerves of the heart

1884–86

Performs research in Breslau with Rudolf Heidenhain and in Leipzig with Karl Ludwig

1890–91

Appointed a professor at the Military-Medical Academy and chief of the physiology division at the Imperial Institute of Experimental Medicine

1890s

Does research with his coworkers on the physiology of digestion

1897

Publishes *Lectures on the Work of the Main Digestive Glands*

1903–36

Does research with his coworkers on the physiology of the higher nervous system

1904

Awarded Nobel Prize in Physiology or Medicine for his contributions to the physiology of digestion

1907
Elected to Russia's Academy of Sciences

1910
Begins construction of the "Towers of Silence"

1914
World War I begins

1917
Overthrow of Tsar Nicholas II and Bolshevik seizure of power

1918–21
Civil War in Russia; Pavlov's son Viktor dies; his son Vsevolod emigrates; Lenin's decree assures Pavlov generous state support

1923
Publishes *Twenty Years of Experience in the Objective Study of the Higher Nervous Activity of Animals*

1924
Leningrad flood almost drowns Pavlov's dogs

1927
Publishes *Lectures on the Work of the Large Hemispheres of the Brain*

1929
Construction begins on the Institute of the Experimental Genetics of Higher Nervous Activity at Koltushi

1932
The apes Roza and Rafael come to Koltushi

1935
Hosts the 15th International Congress of Physiologists in Leningrad

1936
Dies on February 27

acute experiment
An experiment conducted upon an animal either during or immediately after a surgical operation upon it.

chronic experiment
An experiment that begins only after the animal has recovered from an operation upon it.

conditional reflex
A determined relationship between stimulus and response that has been formed through experience, and therefore is changed when the conditions that created it change.

determinism
The view that every event is made inevitable by the events and conditions that proceed it.

differentiation
For Pavlov, the process by which excitation and inhibition combine to distinguish between different stimuli (for example, between two kinds of food).

esophagotomy
A surgical operation that separates the mouth cavity from the digestive tract, so that food swallowed by an animal does not reach the stomach.

eugenics
Francis Galton's term (from the Greek words meaning "well-born") for a science of the development of an improved human type.

excitation
The nervous process by which a stimulus leads to a motor response.

fistula
A thin tube that, when surgically implanted in an organ, brings the secretions of that organ to the surface of the body, where the scientist can analyze them.

gastric glands
The structures in the stomach that produce and secrete gastric juice.

gastric juice

A substance that decomposes food in the stomach and prepares it for absorption in the blood.

heredity

The transmission of characteristics from parents to offspring.

inhibition

The nervous process by which a stimulus slows down or stops a motor response.

isolated stomach

A small division of the stomach that functions normally in response to food, but does not receive the food itself; created by a surgical operation, which Pavlov devised to test the secretory responses of the gastric glands to various foods and stimuli.

materialism

The philosophical view that everything can be explained by the properties of matter.

physiology

The science of vital processes (such as digestion, respiration, and circulation) in the organism.

psychology

The science of behavior and mental processes.

reductionism

The philosophical view that a complex whole can be fully understood by analyzing its simplest parts.

reflex

A determined nervous connection between stimulus and response.

unconditional reflex

An inborn and unvarying relationship between a stimulus and a response.

variable

A factor that might influence the results of an experiment.

vivisection

A scientific procedure involving the dissection or cutting of a living animal.

Works by Ivan Pavlov

Pavlov, Ivan. *Conditioned Reflexes: An Investigation of the Physiological Activity of the Cerebral Cortex.* Translated and edited by G. V. Anrep. 1927. Reprint, New York: Dover, 1960.

———. *Lectures on Conditioned Reflexes: Twenty-five Years of Objective Study of the Higher Nervous Activity (Behaviour) of Animals.* Translated by W. Horsley Gantt. New York: International, 1928.

———. *Psychopathology and Psychiatry.* Translated by D. Myshene and S. Belsky. New Brunswick, N.J.: Transaction, 1994.

———. *The Work of the Digestive Glands.* Translated by W. H. Thompson. London: Griffin, 1902.

Pavlov's life and work

American Psychologist 52, 9 (September 1997). Special issue: "Commemorating Pavlov's Work."

Babkin, B. P. *Pavlov: A Biography.* Chicago: University of Chicago Press, 1949.

Cuny, Hilaire. *Ivan Pavlov: The Man and His Theories.* Translated by Patrick Evans. London: Souvenir, 1964.

European Psychologist 2, 2 (1997). Special issue: "100 Years after Ivan P. Pavlov's *The Work of the Digestive Glands.*"

Gray, Jeffrey. *Ivan Pavlov.* New York: Viking, 1980.

Todes, Daniel P. "Pavlov and the Bolsheviks." *History and Philosophy of the Life Sciences* 17 (December 1995): 379–418.

———. "Pavlov's Physiology Factory." *Isis* 88, 2 (June 1997): 205–46.

History of physiology, psychology, and Russian science

Adams, Mark. "Eugenics in Russia, 1900–1940." In *The Wellborn Science: Eugenics in Germany, France, Brazil, and Russia,* edited by Mark B. Adams. Oxford: Oxford University Press, 1990.

Boakes, Robert. *From Darwin to Behaviourism: Psychology and the Minds of Animals.* Cambridge: Cambridge University Press, 1984.

Boring, Edwin. *A History of Experimental Psychology.* New York: Appleton-Century-Crofts, 1950.

Fearing, Franklin. *Reflex Action: A Study in the History of Physiological Psychology.* New York: Hafner, 1930.

Graham, Loren. *Science in Russia and the Soviet Union: A Short History.* Cambridge: Cambridge University Press, 1993.

Kozulin, Alex. *Psychology in Utopia.* Cambridge: Harvard University Press, 1984.

Krementsov, Nikolai. *Stalinist Science.* Princeton, N.J.: Princeton University Press, 1997.

The history of Russia during Pavlov's lifetime

Ferro, Marc. *Nicholas II: The Last of the Tsars.* New York: Oxford University Press, 1993.

Fitzpatrick, Sheila. *The Russian Revolution.* New York: Oxford University Press, 1982.

Kotkin, Stephen. *Magnetic Mountain: Stalinism as a Civilization.* Berkeley: University of California Press, 1995.

Lincoln, W. Bruce. *The Great Reforms: Autocracy, Bureaucracy, and the Politics of Change in Imperial Russia.* DeKalb: Northern Illinois University Press, 1990.

———. *Passage through Armageddon: The Russians in War and Revolution, 1914–1918.* New York: Simon & Schuster, 1986.

Pipes, Richard. *Russia Under the Bolshevik Regime.* New York: Knopf, 1993.

———. *Russia Under the Old Regime.* New York: Collier, 1992.

Stites, Richard. *Revolutionary Dreams: Utopian Vision and Experimental Life in the Russian Revolution.* New York: Oxford University Press, 1989.

Vogt, George. *Nicholas II.* New York: Chelsea House, 1987.

ACKNOWLEDGMENTS

The author gratefully acknowledges the support of the National
Endowment for the Humanities, Fulbright-Hays, The International
Research and Exchanges Board, and the John Simon Guggenheim
Memorial Foundation; and the assistance of Eleonora Filippova,
Lurii Vinogradov, Vladimir Sobolev, and the coworkers at the
Archive of the Russian Academy of Sciences in St. Petersburg.
Thanks also to the Academy for permission to reproduce the pho-
tos from its collection. Special thanks to Pavlov's granddaughters
and great-granddaughter, Ludmila Balmasova, Maria Sokolova, and
Marina Balmasova.

Archive of the Russian Academy of Sciences, St. Petersburg: 10, 12, 14, 28, 34, 37, 66, 73, 78, 86, 95; Central State Archive of Documentary Films, Photographs, and Sound Recordings of St. Petersburg: 26, 30, 82; from G. H. Lewes, *The Physiology of Common Life*: 8; New York Public Library Picture Collection: 17, 24–25, 27, 80–81, 83; from I. P. Pavlov, *Lectures on the Work of the Main Digestive Glands*: 54, 55; PEANUTS © UFS, Reprinted by Permission: 59; from *Russkii Vrach*, 1907: 40; Reprinted with permission from *Science* and Dr. Michael E. Phelps, Copyright 1985 American Association for the Advancement of Science: 102; from I. M. Sechenov, *Autobiographical Notes*: 20; Daniel Todes: 2, 57, 64, 70, 87, 90–91, 93, 94, 96, 100; The Wellcome Library: 44, 48, 50, 51, 52

Daniel P. Todes is Associate Professor of History of Science, Medicine, and Technology at the Johns Hopkins University. The author of articles and books on the history of science and medicine in Russia, he is currently writing a full-length biography of Ivan Pavlov. His book *Pavlov's Physiology Factory* is forthcoming from the Johns Hopkins University Press in 2001.

Owen Gingerich is Professor of Astronomy and of the History of Science at the Harvard-Smithsonian Center for Astrophysics in Cambridge, Massachusetts. The author of more than 400 articles and reviews, he has also written *The Great Copernicus Chase and Other Adventures in Astronomical History* and *The Eye of Heaven: Ptolomy, Copernicus, Kepler.*